Romero's Legacy

Romero's Legacy

The Call to Peace and Justice

Pilar Hogan Closkey and
John P. Hogan

A SHEED & WARD BOOK

ROWMAN & LITTLEFIELD PUBLISHERS, INC.
Lanham • Boulder • New York • Toronto • Plymouth, UK

A SHEED & WARD BOOK

ROWMAN & LITTLEFIELD PUBLISHERS, INC.

Published in the United States of America
by Rowman & Littlefield Publishers, Inc.
A wholly owned subsidary of The Rowman & Littlefield Publishing Group, Inc.
4501 Forbes Boulevard, Suite 200, Lanham, Maryland 20706
www.rowmanlittlefield.com

Estover Road
Plymouth PL6 7PY
United Kingdom

A revision of chapter 2 is reprinted from *Liturgy and Justice*, courtesy of
Litrugical Press. We gratefully acknowledge prior publication of portions of
chapter 7 in *Notre Dame Magazine*, October 2004.

British Library Cataloguing in Publication Information Available

Library of Congress Cataloging-in-Publication Data
Romero's legacy : the call to peace and justice / [edited by] Pilar Hogan Closkey
    and John P. Hogan.
    p. cm.
    Includes index.
    ISBN-13: 978-0-7425-4821-3 (cloth : alk. paper)
    ISBN-10: 0-7425-4821-X (cloth : alk. paper)
    ISBN-13: 978-0-7425-4822-0 (pbk. : alk. paper)
    ISBN-10: 0-7425-4822-8 (pbk. : alk. paper)
    1. Liberation theology. 2. Church work with the poor. 3. Poverty—Religious
aspects—Christianity. 4. Romero, Oscar A. (Oscar Arnulfo), 1917–1980.
I. Hogan, John P. II. Hogan Closkey, Pilar.
BT83.57.R66 2007
261.8—dc22   2007014078

Printed in the United States of America

♾™ The paper used in this publication meets the minimum requirements of
American National Standard for Information Sciences—Permanence of Paper
for Printed Library Materials, ANSI/NISO Z39.48-1992.

To Msgr. Bob McDermott
and to all the priests, ministers, sisters,
and members of various faith communities
who refuse to give up on Camden

Contents

Foreword

A bishop will die, but the church of God—the people—will never die.

—Archbishop Romero

This volume takes us on a journey of justice, peace, and faith guided by Archbishop Oscar Romero. Each year around the anniversary of his death, March 24, 1980, hundreds of people from around the country—students, lay leaders, pastoral workers, religious educators, teachers, sisters, brothers, and priests—descend on Camden, New Jersey, to attend and participate in the Romero Lecture. This series brings leading theologians and pastoral practitioners to our city to help us read some of the "the signs of our times"—both local and global. The speakers raise issues that cry out for reflection and action: poverty and the growing gap between the rich and poor; war and the growing gaps between nations, cultures, and religions; urban problems; capital punishment; racial discrimination; and immigration.

The last few years have been troubled times for our church and our nation, but as the chapters that follow indicate, it is often in troubled times that we find our strength and our true selves. This truth was vividly portrayed for us in Oscar Romero's living out the paschal mystery of Jesus.

The death of Archbishop Romero is an image that is engraved on the consciousness of many of us, certainly so on mine. The bishop is celebrating the Eucharist at the altar in a simple hospital chapel. He finishes a short homily remembering the dead mother of a friend. Suddenly, a shot rings out; he falls to the floor bleeding profusely. The Eucharistic image is clear—Romero's blood is mixed with that of Christ. That image has become an icon for Christians everywhere. The manner of his death and his martyrdom for the poor and vulnerable remind us of something too often forgotten: Romero's solidarity with the suffering poor of his country grows from and is manifested and celebrated in the church's liturgy.

This relationship of the church's worship to charity and justice is brought out in the chapters that make up this book. In the Eucharist, we can recognize the "other," however different he or she may be from us, and we are called to reach out to him or her. Christ is present in the poor, the homeless, the immigrant, the enemy soldier, and the person on death row. I realize from my own background and experience how hard that statement might be for us to accept, but the Eucharist is a call to make us try. Romero reminds us,

> The Eucharist makes us look back to Calvary twenty centuries ago and beyond that to Moses and the old covenant, an incomparable horizon of history. But it also looks ahead to the future, to the eternal, eschatological, and definitive horizon that presents itself as a demanding ideal. (June 17, 1979)

The issues raised in this volume force us to reexamine what American Catholics might mean by the "option for the poor." As Archbishop Romero's life and death show, to really opt for the poor, with all the meaning that the phrase implies, is no easy task. It will take effort and commitment—both personal and institutional—and it will put us at risk. Nonetheless, more and more, I have come to believe that this might be the price of calling ourselves Catholic Christians.

Without reducing the importance of any of the issues raised here, I would like to make a brief comment on two of them: the plight of our cities and the current debate surrounding immigration. Our urban centers and the people who live in them, especially, the working poor, need our support and assistance. We need healthy and safe cities. No matter where we live, we all depend on urban centers. We need federal, state, urban, and suburban governments, community organizations, civil society, and businesses to pull together to forge fair and equitable regional planning, tax structures, and governance policies.

As for the hot-button questions surrounding immigration, I would simply make a plea for calm and honest discernment. We are a church of immigrants; many of our parents, grandparents, and great-grandparents got off boats from Ireland, Italy, Germany, and Poland. We have been rightly proud of our diverse cultural heritage. Today, again, we are a church of immigrants. We should not be seduced by the partisan arguments about legal versus illegal immigrants. The new immigrants struggle, as did our ancestors, to provide a better life for their families. We need a new approach to immigration policy that is just, fair, and equitable.

However, I am distressed by what I see happening. People who make great sacrifice for their families and contribute to our country's workforce are too often depicted as undesirables, even criminals. This takes away their human dignity. It pains me to see the offspring of European immigrants pushing to pass laws that discriminate against immigrants from Mexico and Central America. Such a stance flies in the face of who we are as a people. Scripture reminds us, "When an alien resides with you in your land, do not molest them. . . . Have the same love for them as for yourselves; for you too were once aliens in the land of Egypt. I, the Lord, am your God" (Leviticus 19:33–34). Latinos carry in their bloodlines and culture a deep sense of the gospel, family, and community. These traits are much needed today by our families, church, and nation. These are our people, indeed; they are us. Again, the Eucharist summons us to responsibility.

Archbishop Romero calls us all and, especially, us bishops to a higher standard—that of Jesus, the Good Shepherd—and he adds another, the standard of his people, especially, the poor. Romero had the humility, ability, and guts to listen to his people, even the poorest, to consult experts, to collaborate, and to seek consensus. He once said that serving and even dying for his people would not be hard, given their love and sacrifice. His life and work were altered by the history in which he lived. He embodied what Pope Benedict XVI describes in *Deus Caritas Est*: "Being Christian is not the result of an ethical choice or a lofty idea, but the encounter with an event, a person which gives life a new horizon and a decisive direction" (no. 1).

In honesty and humility, one needs to admit that Archbishop Romero's example, like that of Jesus, is daunting. But, more important, it is Eucharistic; it calls us to conversion, to risk, to the paschal mystery. As we face that call, it helps to remember the wisdom in the popular prayer dedicated to Romero:

> We cannot do everything and there is a sense of liberation in realizing that.
> . . . We may never see the end results, but that is the difference between the
> master builder and the worker. We are workers, not master builders; ministers, not messiahs. We are prophets of a future not our own.

The lectures collected here are very much in the spirit of Romero's ministry, but they discuss distinctly North American problems and increasingly global problems. I welcome readers to this journey of justice, peace, and faith. The problems are great, but so is our faith.

Joseph A. Galante
Bishop of Camden

Preface

This small volume brings together the annual Romero Lectures presented in Camden, New Jersey, from 2001 through 2007. The lectures are sponsored by the Romero Center, a ministry of Saint Joseph's Pro-Cathedral. They are presented here in the order in which they were delivered and they have been edited, but only to the extent necessary, to translate the spoken word to the written. The editors have tried to convey the spirited conversational tone of the actual event.

The introduction presents the context and the dual background for the lectures: the life and death of Archbishop Oscar Romero and the daily struggles of the people of Camden, one of America's poorest cities. Romero provides the background for the lectures, while poverty and the "option for the poor" are the foreground. His commitment to the poor compels us to look at ourselves. In the richest and most powerful country in history, with the stock market and corporate profits hovering at all-time highs, the gap between the rich and poor grows every day. By some estimates, almost forty million Americans live below the poverty line. One out of every six children and one out of every ten families are poor. About forty-five million Americans have no medical insurance. And yet, we squander thousands of lives and billions of dollars on a preemptive and deceptive war of occupation.

Since 2004, the lectures have been hosted by Rutgers University, in Camden, and have become a significant annual event, involving workshops, panel discussions, and films that focus on and debate the issues raised by the speakers. We hope that those discussions might be continued in parish adult education programs and college and high school classrooms. Discussion questions and a list of resources have been appended to each chapter to facilitate that process.

There are many people who should be thanked for the work that has gone into the lectures and the preparation of this volume. First and foremost, we thank Larry DiPaul, director of the Romero Center, and his staff and board who have worked hard to iron out every detail to ensure the success of the lectures; and we especially thank Omar Aguilar, Meghan Allen, Msgr. William Brennan, Sean Closkey, Sean Dolan, Michael Giansiracusa, Joe Glass, Fr. Kenneth Hallahan, Kevin Hickey, Clare Hogan, Tom Jennings, John Klein, Tom Lynch, Msgr. Roger McGrath, Fr. George McLean, OMI, Kevin Moran, Fr. Terry Odien, John Pallies, Dino Pinto, Frederick Pratt, Brian Reavey, Teresa Reyes, Sr. Nancy Roche, SSJ, Pat Slater, Clare Strockbine, Sean Sanford, Barbara Thomas, and Sr. Clarisa Vazquez, SSJ.

A special note of gratitude is expressed to provost Roger Dennis and his staff for the support of Rugters University for hosting the lectures. We also thank St. Pius X Parish and St. Mary's Parish for hosting earlier lectures. We are grateful for the dedication and support of various faith communities and community organizations, especially, Camden Churches Organized for People, Concerned Black Clergy, and Saint Joseph's Carpenter Society.

A special note of thanks is expressed to Maura Donohue for her careful and creative editorial assistance. Our thanks are also owed to the editors at Rowman & Littlefield for their patient guidance in bringing this volume to publication. All royalties earned on this book will be donated to Saint Joseph's Pro-Cathedral ministries.

We express gratitude to Bishop Joseph Galante for his foreword to the volume and for his support of the Romero Center and Saint Joseph's Pro-Cathedral Parish. Most importantly, we thank Msgr. Bob McDermott, the inspiration behind the Romero Center and the other ministries of Saint Joseph's. With gratitude for his unswerving support for the people of Camden, we dedicate this book to him.

Finally, the editors thank Liturgical Press for permission to republish a revised version of "People of Faith and Global Citizens: Eucharist and Globalization" from *Liturgy and Justice: To Worship God in Spirit and Truth*, (2002), edited by Anne Y. Koester, as chapter 2. We also acknowledge prior publication and are grateful for the permission to republish parts of chapter 7 from *Notre Dame Magazine* (October 2004).

Introduction

Romero's Vision and the City Parish—Urban Ministry and Urban Planning

Pilar Hogan Closkey and John P. Hogan

DANGEROUS MEMORY

In a city such as Camden, New Jersey, where one out of every ten houses is boarded up and abandoned, "an empty building cries out for rebirth." Thus, Msgr. Robert McDermott, pastor of Saint Joseph's Pro-Cathedral, decided in the early 1990s that the vacant convent should be put to use for the people of the city. Camden is often described as the poorest city in America, located in the country's richest state. That irony is not lost on McDermott or the struggling people of the city.

The Catholic roots in Camden are old and deep, as they are in many urban centers of our nation. Indeed, as scholars have pointed out, the missionary endeavor of the early church was largely an urban venture. "Paul was a city person. The city speaks through his language" (Meeks, *The First Urban Christians*, 9). He was proud of his urban working-class identity and that he was a "citizen of no mean city" (Acts 21:39). As his letters indicate, the message spread via a network of cities—from Jerusalem to Caesarea, Antioch, Rome, Carthage, and Alexandria. Nonetheless, in the last forty years, the church has become decidedly middle class and suburban. Meanwhile, our cities, to a great extent, have become magnets for the poor, minorities, and immigrants.

McDermott, known to all as Father Bob, heard the call not only to respond to the needs of his East Camden parishioners but also to expose the wider Catholic community and other faith communities, especially, young people, to the plight of cities like Camden. "We want young people to see that there is both opportunity and challenge in the work of the

1

church. We want all Catholics to understand their role in bringing about a societal commitment to end poverty and discrimination in our world." The old convent was resurrected into an urban retreat center, and it opened on March 24, 1998, the anniversary of the martyrdom of Archbishop Oscar Romero. Since then, almost ten thousand people, mainly, college and high school students, have participated in social justice and spirituality programs at the Romero Center.

Archbishop Romero was the perfect patron. As his friend and advisor, Jon Sobrino, SJ, put it, "he took both God and the world seriously." He incarnated the church and made it a church that acts in history and acts in and with the poor. In Romero's own words,

> The poor tell us what the world is and what service the church can offer the world. The poor tell us what the *polis*—the city—is, and what it means for the church to live in the world. . . .
>
> In the first place, we are incarnated in the poor; we want a church that is shoulder to shoulder with the poor people of El Salvador. Every time we come closer to the poor, we discover the true face of the suffering servant of Yahweh. There we come closer to knowing the mystery of Christ who becomes human and becomes poor through us (*Martyr's Message*, 82).

Each year, around the anniversary of Romero's death, the Romero Center sponsors a day of discussion and reflection focusing on a lecture that integrates Christian faith and the quest for social justice and peace. The lectures illustrate the solidarity between the poor and the nonpoor to which Baptism and Eucharist call us. They resonate with the Gospel call to justice and charity, Catholic social teaching, and the church's preferential option for the poor.

As the title of this work indicates, the chapters that follow highlight the living legacy of Archbishop Romero, his life, love, and commitment. But more importantly, the chapters evoke what Kevin Burke, SJ, calls the "heart of the matter" "the memory of Romero," "the memory of suffering" (see "The Future of the Church"). Romero reminds us of "the dangerous memory of Christ's suffering-unto-God that not only nourishes the church with daily bread, but guides the church in its prophetic service of the future of the world."

The living legacy of Romero, like the memory of Romero, is therefore not about things past. It is rather a remembering that makes us look for what is to come. It is the Eucharistic and eschatological memory of the hoped-for kingdom of God. Throughout his life and, especially, his episcopal ministry, Romero remembered and lived the paschal mystery: the life, death, and resurrection of Jesus. This *dangerous memory* (the term is from Johann Baptist Metz, SJ) was his life's blood, animating him, even in the face of imminent death. In Romero, "we encounter a bishop for a new millennium, a bishop attuned to the way the future is built, brick by brick, from the sufferings of the past, a bishop who leads a church focused not on itself, its truth or purity, but focused on the poor and their future with God, where every tear will be wiped away" (Burke, "The Future of the Church," 13).

Burke further summarizes this profound insight: "The vision of Archbishop Romero and the dangerous memory of faith that awakened that vision in him can touch each of us. It calls us to remember, to tell stories, and to celebrate" (1–2). That dangerous memory of Jesus is precisely what we reenact and celebrate at every Eucharist. It calls us all to build the future of the church. Being a Catholic Christian is not a passive acceptance; it demands an active involvement in history. Living the faith means taking risks, but it also brings joy and hope as well as small steps in building the reign of justice, peace, and love announced by Jesus. That is a large part of the "this" in "Do this in remembrance of me." That is the dangerous memory of Archbishop Romero.

ROMERO: FINDING GOD IN THE POOR

In 1974, Oscar Romero became bishop of Santiago de María, El Salvador. In 1977, he was the surprise choice to succeed the highly regarded Archbishop Luis Chávez y González, who had been archbishop of San Salvador since 1938. Chávez was a staunch defender of the poor and had championed the causes of Vatican II and Medellín. Romero, however, was considered a safe choice who had been critical of progressive nuns and priests. Fr. Ignacio Martin-Baró, SJ, one of the Jesuits murdered in 1989 at the University of Central America, sums up the reaction to the selection:

> When news came from Rome that Bishop Romero had been chosen to succeed Archbishop Chávez, the Salvadoran government and oligarchy were jubilant. They were certain they had won a great victory for the conservative cause. . . . For their part, a good number of clergy of the Archdiocese received the news of his appointment with dejection and apprehension. They regarded it as a sign that Rome seemed more concerned to maintain good relations with the government than to serve the needs of the Christian community in El Salvador. (quoted in Romero, *Voice of the Voiceless*, 4–5)

That reaction had to be quickly altered. Right after he became archbishop, government troops opened fire on a group of peasants protesting in the main plaza of the capital. Soon after, Romero's friend, Fr. Rutilio Grande, SJ, was gunned down by hired thugs because of his defense of the poor. During this period, six priests were assassinated by death squads.

Romero played down the idea that he underwent a deep conversion; he called it an "evolution." It is clear nonetheless that a profound transformation took place in him and how he saw his role. He became the "voice of the voiceless" and defended his activist priests and the poor. He sought out and listened to advice from all quarters. He was convinced that the Spirit was speaking through the sufferings of the poor.

The new archbishop forged a pastoral team—pastors, catechists, lay leaders, and scholars, usually, Jesuits from the university. This team assisted him with his diocesan planning, homilies, and messages. His legacy is summarized in his homilies, his four pastoral letters, and a few other major addresses. Each of the letters responds to specific needs and gives voice to the poor. His homilies, broadcast to the nation via the diocesan radio station YSAX, consisted of reflections on the Scripture readings for the day and a discussion of the events of the past week. In strong terms, he denounced injustice and announced hope.

During this period, El Salvador was embroiled in a civil war that would kill over seventy-five thousand people—mostly from among the poor. The military, supported by the U.S. government, backed wealthy landowners in their efforts to suppress all grassroots movements. Romero, however, strongly supported popular community organizations. "He admired the justice of their struggle, the moral weight of their cause. . . . He was convinced that 'even outside the church's precincts, Christ's redemption has great power, and peoples struggling for freedom, even though they are not Christian, are inspired by the Spirit of Jesus'" (*Voice of the Voiceless*, 45).

He publicly condemned both the killing of the innocent and the political system that supported it. Nonetheless, he remained humble and did not shy away from criticism of himself or the church. "For at a time of national crisis those of us who feel it our duty to denounce the sin that lies at the root of the crisis ought also to be ready to be criticized so as to bring about our own conversion and to build up a church that can be, for our own people, what Vatican II defines as 'the national sacrament of salvation'" (*Voice of the Voiceless*, 125).

In spite of his efforts to open dialogue with government and military leaders and the wealthy, his stance provoked fierce opposition. His opponents were not only the ruling economic and military powers but even fellow bishops. Some of the latter sought to have him removed from his archdiocese. This reaction was particularly hurtful to Romero. In February 1980, he went to Belgium to receive an honorary doctorate from Louvain University, and he proceeded on to Rome to seek the support of Pope John Paul II.

He gave me a chance to present my thought and he also expressed his views . . . Although my first impression was not satisfactory, I believe it was a most useful visit and talk, since he was very frank, and I have learned that one should not always expect a resounding approval, but rather it is more useful to receive admonitions that can improve our work (*Voice of the Voiceless*, 167).

Discouraged but not broken, he recalled that John Paul had recommended boldness and courage along with patience and balance—a stance with which he completely agreed.

On his return, he wrote to President Carter asking him to cut off military aid to El Salvador. This intensified opposition from many quarters. In the face of this mounting opposition, he continued to live his life within the context of Eucharistic and eschatological hope. He clearly seemed to know that he was a target.

On Sunday, March 23, 1980, he preached for the last time in the cathedral. His homily was wide-ranging, and it showed the depth of his relationship with his people. He spoke for over an hour, unfolding the Scripture texts for the fourth Sunday in Lent. His main theme was human dignity and liberation—personal, social, and transcendent. He touched on practical issues, such as the advancement of women, the negative impact of *machismo*, and the need for the church to be open to change. Toward the end of the homily, he turned to the events of the week. The repression and killings of the poor and priests weighed on his heart. He appealed to the civil government, the military, and the wealthy, but he spoke directly to soldiers, national guardsmen, and police. He begged them, he ordered them, to stop the killing (Romero, *Voice of the Voiceless*, 18).

The next day Archbishop Romero was murdered while celebrating Mass. To the end, he was the good shepherd, killed for his flock. He never gave up on his people or even on their enemies. He never gave up on the dangerous memory of Jesus. He never gave up on the future of the church, but he clearly understood the cost of discipleship. "To follow faithfully the pope's magisterium in theory is very easy. But when you try to live those teachings, try to incarnate them, try to make them reality in the history of a suffering people like ours—that is when conflicts arise" (Pelton, *Archbishop Romero*, 78).

His faithful grasp of the future was so strong that two weeks before his death, he had already forgiven his killers. "If they kill me, I will rise again in the people of El Salvador. . . . You can tell them, if they succeed in killing me, that I pardon them, and I bless those who may carry out the killing. But I wish that they could realize that they are wasting their time. A bishop will die, but the church of God—the people—will never die" (*Voice of the Voiceless*, 50–51).

SAINT JOSEPH'S—EAST CAMDEN

At first glance, San Salvador might seem a long way from Camden, New Jersey. But perhaps not when two points emerge: first, the impact of long-term poverty, powerlessness, and violence on a people; and, second, the staying power and spirit of committed faith communities. These two factors provide a common ground. So, after noting something of the struggle of El Salvador's people, we now turn briefly to Camden and particularly to Saint Joseph's parish in East Camden.

Amid boarded-up houses, deadening unemployment, high infant mortality rates, and out-of-control drug markets, Msgr. Bob McDermott responded to this dire situation by linking pastoral ministry to urban planning and renewal. He took up tasks involving community organizing, affordable housing, education, and jobs. Crime, drugs, and the incarceration of too many young men were burning issues. Such issues were linked to worship, learning, and service at the parish level. The priest pulled together pastors and congregations from all over the city and organized to build a better future. The churches of Camden—all denominations—have not given up on their people and have made strong contributions to rebuilding the city. Indeed, the churches have become the last bastion of hope. The hope holds, but the uphill struggle continues.

Camden's population has plummeted since the end of World War II, from about 120,000 to fewer than 80,000 today. A once-vibrant working-class city with large employers such as Campbell Soup, RCA Victor, and the New York Shipbuilding Corporation, Camden has now become a holding zone for the working poor—minorities, immigrants, and older residents, unwilling or unable to move out. The city is 57 percent African American and 40 percent Hispanic, with small groups of Asians and whites. The number of new Mexican immigrants is increasing. Forty-four percent of residents live below the poverty line, the highest rate in the country. The median annual income is about $18,000, a stark contrast with the $61,672 for the state of New Jersey (*New York Times*, November 5, 2006). Illiteracy and addictions are rampant, as is the widespread breakdown of family. Over 50 percent of Camden's children live in poverty, three times the state average. Almost 40 percent of residents are nineteen or younger, but only 50 percent of those graduate from high school. Boarded-up buildings and drug markets mar the cityscape. There is only one full-service supermarket and no movie theaters. The city ranks first in poverty and fifth in crime in the United States. The ironic aspect of this dismal snapshot is compounded by the fact that Camden is surrounded by relatively affluent suburbs.

This sad commentary, however, does not tell the full story. In fact, it disfigures the true face of Camden. Indeed, a dangerous paschal and Eucharistic memory lingers on in the struggles of Camden's churches. Saint Joseph's Pro-Cathedral in East Camden is the focal point for bringing people together. Urban plight and flight, education, affordable housing, police-community relations, crime and drugs, government corruption, and job training have become integrated into the urban ministry of Saint Joseph's and surrounding congregations. The church's social teachings on participation, solidarity, subsidiarity, and the option for the poor are the defining principles (Hogan, "Taking a City off the Cross," 45–63). Pope John Paul's "Ecclesia in America" presents the challenge. His words fit well as both a description of Camden and the commitment of Romero.

> Also on the increase in America is the phenomenon of urbanization. . . . The frequent lack of planning in this process is a source of many evils. . . . As the Synod Fathers pointed out, "in certain cases, some urban areas are like islands where violence, juvenile delinquency, and an air of desperation flourish." . . . The evangelization of urban culture is a formidable challenge for the church (no. 21).

> Sacred Scripture reminds us that God hears the cry of the poor (cf. Ps 34:7), and the Church must heed the cry of those most in need. Hearing their voice, she must live with the poor and share their distress. By her lifestyle, her priorities, her words and her actions, she must testify that she is in communion and solidarity with them (no. 8).

This challenge and commitment are exemplified in the priests, sisters, teachers, staff, and people of Saint Joseph's. In a city that suffers from almost every social ill, a group of dedicated community residents has formed that is willing to stay and invest itself in the betterment of its neighborhoods and the city at large.

The Saint Joseph's Carpenter Society was founded in 1985 as a nonprofit affordable-housing program. The program provides homeownership opportunities for the working poor and seeks to invigorate and stabilize disinvested neighborhoods. One out of every eight houses in the area was abandoned; almost 70 percent were rental units; many were havens for drug dealers. Crime, isolation, and fear ruled the streets. Saint Joseph's took on the boarded-up blocks, the drug dealers, and government housing agencies, at all levels. The Carpenter Society set out to rehabilitate abandoned housing units and sell them to qualified owners. A required education program is provided for all potential homeowners in the financial management skills necessary to not only purchase a house but also to sustain it. At present, the education program trains three hundred people per year.

By early 2007, almost seven hundred units of affordable, safe, and healthy homes have been provided for families. The Carpenter Society has become the most productive nonprofit housing provider in New Jersey. The *Philadelphia Inquirer* (February 2, 2007) reports,

> Since the Carpenter Society's founding in 1985, it's been chipping away at Camden's vexing housing problem. It initially worked on one house at a time—raising money, bringing in volunteers, and selling the fixed-up homes for cost of materials, less what was raised. The society soon hired paid workers, fixing one block at a time. Now it can rebuild an entire neighborhood. . . . The results have been stunning.

A critical element in Saint Joseph's urban ministry involves community organizing. McDermott was one of the founding members of Camden Churches Organized for People, a faith-based coalition comprising thirty congregations. This effort has proven essential for leadership training and participation of people in decision making, neighborhood control, and community-planning strategies. In 2002, the organization, working closely with Concerned Black Clergy, spearheaded the drive for the state-sponsored Camden Recovery Act (Gillette, *Camden after the Fall*, 193–215; Hogan, "Taking a City off the Cross," 49–61). That struggle continues with efforts to filter some of the state funds down to local neighborhoods. Camden Churches Organized for People has also sought to reach out in solidarity to surrounding suburban congregations to expose them and interest them in the plight of the city.

Public education in Camden, as in many urban centers, is in disarray. Catholic schools, however, fight simply to survive. Saint Joseph's Elementary School, which has functioned for over one hundred years, was scheduled for closure in 1985. Since that time, however, it has grown to 285 students and has also grown in support both from the diocese and from outside funding sources and benefactors. In a city where less than 50 percent of the students in public schools graduate from high school and about 10 percent go on to college, Saint Joseph's, a multicultural school that reflects the local community, provides a sharp contrast. More than 95 percent of graduates finish high school and 85 percent go on to college.

Camden's urban ministry received another vital component, with the opening of the Romero Center. Urban change and development do not take place in isolation. Cities such as Camden had become scapegoats in the sense of Leviticus 16. Urban centers have had "the sinful faults and transgressions" (Leviticus 16:21) of their neighbors heaped onto them. As a city planner working in Camden in 2002 pointed out, "the city has absorbed the prisoners, the garbage, the raw sewage, and the unwanted polluting industries for the whole area and really receives little or no remuneration. The surrounding area could never reimburse the city for the service it provides" (Hogan, "Taking a City off the Cross," 61). In a very real sense, our cities do our heavy lifting and carry off our sins.

McDermott recognized this and saw the need to raise awareness among suburbanites about the effects of social policy on cities such as Camden. As the Brookings Institute points out,

> A large body of research has demonstrated that concentrated poverty exacts multiple costs on individuals and society. These costs come in the form of: reduced private-sector investment and local job opportunities; increased prices for the poor; higher levels of crime; negative impacts on mental and physical health; low-quality neighborhood schools; and heavy burdens on local governments that induce out-migration of middle-class households. Together, these factors combine to limit the life chances and quality of life available to residents of high-poverty neighborhoods (quoted in Catholic Charities USA, "Poverty in America," 13).

Charity, as important as it is, is not enough. Education for justice becomes an imperative. Structures that create poverty must be challenged and changed. But the experience, understanding, judgment, and action that process demands need guidance and reflection. In late 1997 and early 1998, the Romero Center, housed in the old convent, took shape. The center, as noted, provides retreats to college and high school students and others as well. Urban plunge and journey-to-justice-type retreats expose participants to daily life in Camden. By spending time and sharing meals with the working poor, retreatants are moved from harboring stereotypical images to effecting compassionate action. Those who come to serve are in fact served. Personal stories are shared, and hopes and aspirations are compared. Participants are guided by the center staff through the pastoral cycle of experience, social analysis, theological reflection, and action that allows them to process what they have seen and heard in light of gospel values, Catholic social teaching, and the church's option for the poor.

The reaction of participants and parents to the experience has been overwhelmingly positive: "My son returned from the Romero Center yesterday. He spoke for two hours about his urban challenge experience." "My daughter never had a personal conversation with a homeless person before. Since she came back from Camden, she looks at life differently. I hope it lasts." One mother summed up the impact by saying, "I want to thank you for making [my son's] experience such a positive and rewarding one. Weeks later, he continues to talk about it. Not only were his eyes opened, but his spirit was challenged and a confidence that he could make a difference was affirmed." It appears that some of these young people have heeded Archbishop Romero's call and have begun to open themselves to the poor and grasp, a little at least, of what an option for the poor might mean in our country today.

The Romero Center has expanded into parish-based justice and peace education programs for the whole diocese. Programs for adult leaders, priests, religious, and deacons have also been established. It is from these pastoral experiences and reflection on the experiences that the annual Romero Lecture has emerged.

OVERVIEW OF CHAPTERS

Although the chapters that follow are meant as calls to solidarity, they also raise controversial issues that are often the cause of bitter divisions. For that reason, a few brief comments on method might be of assistance. The authors help us to see how intertwined the issues really are. They also provide perspective by viewing these issues from the same fundamental horizon: all begin with the premise of a God, who loves us in spite of our best efforts to cauterize ourselves from that love. This hermeneutical light directs the reader to a Christian ethic of human relatedness and right relationships that is profound and personal but open and transcendent. "He who does not love does not know God; for God is love" (1 John 4:8).

The beam from that light is reflected through the prism of Catholic social principles: the inherent dignity in simply being a human person; the call to family and community and the participation, solidarity, and subsidiarity that such a call entails; the rights and reciprocal responsibilities of individuals and communities that are demanded by our complex global society; the option for the poor and vulnerable; the dignity and respect for work and the rights of workers; and the environmental concern and care for God's creation. The principles cohere and are given teeth through a process of faith-based community organizing.

The authors remind us of our relatedness, experienced through the Spirit in our midst, the sacramental imagination, and the common future to which the Father and Jesus call us all. But they add to our discomfit by reminding us that sin is settling for the world that we inherit, for the world as it is, for business as usual. Clearly, our authors are people who stand "askew to the world" (McCabe, *What Is Ethics All About?* 155). Indeed, they are out of step, as Romero was, not because they identify with the past, but because they identify with the future. Their stance is Eucharistic and eschatological. They bring alive that profound insight attributed to St. Augustine: "Hope has two beautiful daughters: anger and courage. Anger at the way things are in the world and courage to make them better." With Romero as guide and Camden's struggle as incentive, the authors trigger a dangerous memory that pushes us to reach out and reach up to a different future.

Each chapter certainly reflects on Romero's legacy. But, our subtitle, *The Call to Peace and Justice*, is deliberately meant to provoke the hard questions behind the "dangerous memory" that he evoked. Given the current historical context, with both church and state facing major crises, is it possible for the American church to heed the call and move to a "preferential option for the poor"? How can we as a faith community and institution go beyond high-sounding slogans and incarnate the church's social teachings? Are we willing to push back at our consumer society? What is at stake? What are the risks? What do we value? What do we really love? The chapters of this book lead us to these kinds of questions. In these difficult times of terrorism, war, and scandal, they challenge us, the church, the wounded body of Christ to rebuild trust and be a sign of the kingdom of peace and justice announced by Jesus.

In chapter 1, "In the Footsteps of Martyrs: Lesson from Central America" (2001), Robert McDermott sets the stage for the lectures. Inspired by a Maryknoll-sponsored retreat to Central America, he reflects on the ministry of Romero and the other Central American martyrs to invigorate his own vision of the urban parish and the role of the Romero Center.

Chapter 2, "The Eucharist and Social Justice" (2002), by John Hogan, discusses the Eucharist in terms of "relational wholeness." He puts emphasis on the presence of Christ in the community and in the struggle for a just and peaceful world.

In chapter 3, Bishop Thomas Gumbleton teases out the powerful words of Pope Paul VI, "If you want peace, work for justice" (2003). Global poverty, an unjust global economic order, and the preemptive, unjust war of occupation in Iraq are framed in the context of "structural social injustice"—what John Paul II called "structures of violence."

Chapter 4, "Liberation Theology for the Twenty-First Century" (2004) by Gustavo Gutiérrez, presents a profound, personal, and practical reflection on the "preferential option for the poor" and how that option should be placed at the center of Catholic theology at the dawn of the new millennium. Exposing the falsehood in empty gestures and slogans, Gutiérrez confronts us with the question of whether and how we can honestly tell poor people that God loves them. His response to that question contains the beginnings of a theology of "true freedom, liberation, and joy."

In chapter 5, "Dead Men Walking: The Journey Continues" (2005), Sr. Helen Prejean, with passion and humor, takes us on her personal journey of "awakening" and invites us into her campaign to see through the vindictiveness and scapegoating involved in capital punishment. The death penalty is expensive, ineffective as a deterrent, and is used disproportionately against the poor and minorities. Officially condemned by the church and especially by Pope John Paul II, that teaching has been long ignored by most American Catholics.

Chapter 6, "The Color of Money: Racism and the Economy" (2006), by Diana Hayes, draws the reader into a historical, ethical, and theological discussion of the failed efforts at economic opportunity for black Americans, especially women. She take us from the New Deal, through the civil rights movement, to the present. She also indicates the failed promise of the U.S. bishops' pastoral *Economic Justice for All*. In spite of these efforts, racism is still the poison at the bottom of the American well. Hayes evokes the memory and dream of Martin Luther King Jr., who, like Romero, spoke truth to power and condemned the greed and selfishness embedded in racism, consumerism, and classism.

Chapter 7, "A Promised Land, A Devil's Highway: The Crossroads of the Undocumented Immigrant" (2007), is by Daniel Groody. He brings us deeper into the dangerous memory of Jesus and accompanies us along the rough road traveled by undocumented immigrants. As our nation threatens to enact criminal laws and build ever higher and longer walls to keep out workers that it needs, Christians and the Catholic church in particular will have to face tough decisions. Can we celebrate the Eucharist and at the same time support barriers of physical and spiritual exclusion? Do we continue to help immigrants, especially, the undocumented, and fight for a fair and just immigration policy, or do we deny a mandate so central to our tradition "to welcome the stranger."

While the U.S. church has an unparalleled track record in charity and service, what the concepts of peace, justice, and the "option for the poor" mean in our complex capitalistic democracy is far from clear. The issues raised here and the gospel call in our subtitle point to the need for creative leadership, pastoral vision, and a liberating spirituality that summon the whole church to bear witness to real social change and stand with the poor. As Pope Benedict reminds us, we "cannot and must not remain on the sidelines in the fight for justice" (*Deus Caritas Est*, no. 28a).

Archbishop Romero, in his own context, provides an inspiring model. The following chapters take small steps in the direction of that model.

DISCUSSION QUESTIONS

1. What did the "dangerous memory" of Jesus mean for Romero? What might it mean for American Catholics today?
2. Discuss the principles of solidarity, subsidiarity, and option for the poor in light of Camden's situation. Can you think of examples in your area where these principles might apply?
3. Does your state have an urban policy? What do you think should go into such policies? Do you think neighboring counties or suburbs have any responsibility for the plight of inner cities?

NOTE

For an excellent nationwide program in faith and justice education, go to www
.justfaith.org. For information on the Romero Center, go to www.romero-center
.org.

RESOURCES AND FURTHER STUDY

Benedict XVI. *Deus Caritas Est.* Libreria Editrice Vaticana (Vatican Publishing
    House). www.vatican.va/holy_father/benedict_xvi/encyclicals/documents/
    hf_ben-xvi_enc_20051225_deus-caritas-est_en.html, 2005 (accessed May 2,
    2007).
Brockman, James R. *Romero: A Life.* Maryknoll, N.Y.: Orbis Books, 2005.
Burke, Kevin F. "The Future of the Church in the Memory of Romero." In *Arch-
    bishop Romero: Martyr and Prophet for the New Millennium,* edited by Robert Pel-
    ton, 1–15. Scranton, Penn.: University of Scranton Press, 2006.
Catholic Charities USA. "Poverty in America: A Threat to the Common Good."
    Policy paper, Alexandria, Va., August 30, 2006. www.catholiccharitiesusa.org/
    poverty/downloads/policy06.pdf (accessed May 2, 2007).
Closkey, Sean, and Pilar Hogan. "Building Houses, Educating Communities: A
    Praxis Model." *Living Light* 35 (Summer 1999): 38–44.
Cronin, Brian. *Value Ethics: A Lonergan Perspective.* Nairobi, Kenya: Consolata In-
    stitute of Philosophy Press, 2006.
Gillette, Howard, Jr. *Camden after the Fall: Decline and Renewal in a Post-industrial
    City.* Philadelphia: University of Pennsylvania Press, 2005.
Hogan, John P. "Taking a City off the Cross: Camden Churches Organized for Peo-
    ple." Chapter 3 of *Credible Signs of Christ Alive: Case Studies from the Catholic Cam-
    paign for Human Development.* Lanham, Md.: Sheed and Ward, 2003.
Jacobsen, Dennis A. *Doing Justice: Congregations and Community Organizing.* Min-
    neapolis, Minn.: Fortress Press, 2001.
John Paul II. "Ecclesia in America." *Origins* 28 (February 4, 1999): 566–92.
Massaro, Thomas. *Living Justice: Catholic Social Teaching in Action.* Franklin, Ind.:
    Sheed and Ward, 2000.
McCabe, Herbert. *What Is Ethics All About? A Re-evaluation of Law, Love, and Lan-
    guage.* Washington, D.C.: Corpus Books, 1969.
Meeks, Wayne A. *The First Urban Christians: The Social World of the Apostle Paul.*
    New Haven, Conn.: Yale University Press, 1983.
Pelton, Robert, ed. *Archbishop Romero: Martyr and Prophet for the New Millennium.*
    Scranton, Penn.: University of Scranton Press, 2006. Also available from Uni-
    versity of Scranton Press are DVD and VHS versions of *Archbishop Romero: Mar-
    tyr and Prophet for the New Millennium,* Stepstone Productions, St. Louis, Mo.
Ramsey, Meredith. "Redeeming the City: Exploring the Relationship between
    Church and Metropolis." *Urban Affairs Review* 33 (May 5, 1998): 595–626.
Romero, Oscar. *A Martyr's Message: Six Homilies of Archbishop Oscar Romero.* Kansas
    City: Celebration Books, 1981.

———. *Voice of the Voiceless: The Four Pastoral Letters and Other Statements*. Maryknoll, N.Y.: Orbis Books, 1992.

Toton, Suzanne C. *Justice Education: From Service to Solidarity*. Milwaukee, Wis.: Marquette University Press, 2006.

Wood, Richard. *Faith in Action: Religion, Race, and Democratic Organizing in America*. Chicago: University of Chicago Press, 2002.

1

In the Footsteps of Martyrs:
Lessons from Central America

Robert T. McDermott

Archbishop Oscar Romero of El Salvador provided a clear model of personal conversion as someone who not only dedicated his life to the poor and oppressed but also invited, even demanded, others to join him.

Archbishop Romero calls all of us to change sinful structures. We must not only address our personal acts of sinfulness but also challenge structural and social sinfulness. The recent opening of the Romero Center in Camden, New Jersey, provides a vehicle for just this kind of personal conversion, moving us from acts of simple charity and service to a life dedicated to justice and changing structures that oppress the poor.

I would like to share with you some reflections on the recent pilgrimage—a kind of moving retreat—that I made to Central America. It was "moving" in at least two ways—first, it personally moved me in a deep and spiritual way, and second, the pilgrimage to the many shrines of the Central American martyrs moved our group all over El Salvador and Guatemala. The experience, for me, was like a visit to the Holy Land. I felt like I was walking on sacred ground. I felt this way because that part of the world has truly been a land of martyrs, not only because of the long line of murdered priests, bishops, sisters, and lay leaders but also because of the holiness of the poor—the *campesinos* and *barrio* dwellers—whom I saw and met. The poor were truly the victimized. In Central America, I was profoundly reminded that in our tradition—summed up in the paschal mystery of Jesus—the victim has the last word.

First, I recount something of this moving experience—the people I met and the places visited. This will re-create the context out of which I took some valuable lessons. Second, concentrating on the ministry of Oscar

15

Romero, I draw out of this spiritual journey something of his theological and pastoral vision and some lessons that I believe are applicable to the church anywhere. The lessons stretch from learning to leadership to liturgy and laity. Finally, I try to draw some tentative conclusions for our church life here in Camden and, indeed, for linking our local church— with our own problems of suffering and poverty—to the suffering and poverty around the globe.

Indeed, this trip awakened me to the plight of our sisters and brothers around the world. But it also awakened in me a healthy sense of guilt for not having been more aware of that plight early on and of my own country's complicity in it.

WALKING ON SACRED GROUND

In January 2001, I joined a number of American priests for a Maryknoll-sponsored retreat to Central America. In a very real sense, it was more of a pilgrimage for me than a retreat. I had long read about the suffering and martyrdom that have recently marked the church in Central America— finally, I had a chance to see it firsthand. Visiting the shrines of the martyrs, I was overwhelmed with a sense of the sacred. It broadened my horizons—big time. Honestly, I will never be the same.

While in Salvador, we conversed with people who worked closely with Archbishop Romero, Fr. Rutilio Grande, SJ, the four martyred American religious women, and the Jesuits who were murdered, along with their housekeeper and her daughter. I return to some of that bloody history later.

In Guatemala, we visited the site where Bishop Juan José Gerardi was brutally murdered in his own rectory. It was no coincidence that just forty-eight hours before the bishop was bludgeoned to death, the Human Rights Commission of this archdiocese, which he chaired, published its final report documenting the massive violation of human rights in Guatemala. For over twenty years, military-lead repression caused the death or disappearance of some two hundred thousand people, mostly comprising poor Mayan Indians and including thousands of women and children.

We also journeyed to Santiago Atilán to visit the place of service and martyrdom of Fr. Stan Rother. Guatemalan armed forces killed Father Rother, an American priest from Oklahoma, because of his outspoken criticism of the military violence and abuse of the people in his rural parish. The warm and friendly Mayan people were swept up in the maze of military violence that had ravaged Guatemala since the 1950s but had escalated dramatically in the 1970s. Father Stan became their only protector, and for that, he died. It is clear that the people consider Father Stan a saint. It was explained to us that in a fascinating Mayan tradition that although Stan's body was taken back to the United States for burial, his heart—literally, his heart—was retained by the people of his parish and is now encased in a memorial in their church. The memorial is surrounded by hundreds of small crosses signifying parishioners killed by the army.

One particular scene stood out for me. We were in the cathedral in Guatemala City. On the cement wall outside the cathedral were inscribed the names of ninety thousand people who lost their lives. People streamed in and out of the church and offered their silent prayers before a huge cross with the black corpse of Jesus—the Cross of Esquipulas. This cross signifies the coming together of the Central American countries and the suffering imitation of Christ that its people have gone through. I was touched deeply by this global image of the poor, drawn together in their suffering and dying like Jesus—the victim.

While in El Salvador, I had the opportunity to come to know Monsignor Urioste who was friend and vicar-general to Archbishop Romero. I also met Fr. John Spain, a Maryknoll priest who worked closely with Romero and took the place of Father Grande after he was murdered. We met Sr. Terry Anderson, MM, who worked with the four American women—two Maryknoll sisters, Maura Clark and Ita Ford, one Ursuline sister, Dorothy Kazel, and a lay missionary, Jean Donovan—who were raped and murdered on the road from the airport to San Salvador by Salvadoran soldiers on December 2, 1980.

At the Jesuit University of Central America, we spoke at length with Fr. Dean Brackley, SJ, an American Jesuit who volunteered to help fill the gap left by the murder of Jesuit priest faculty members who were killed by a military death squad in 1989. They died because of their strong support for the poor, their writings against oppression, and because they had been advisors of Oscar Romero.

The most moving experiences for me were our visits to the scenes of Romero's life and death. We saw his place of burial in the crypt of San Salvador Cathedral, and we celebrated Mass at the altar where he was shot. That concelebrated Mass was one of the most profound moments of my life. I reflected, as very likely, Archbishop Romero had reflected, that just as torture was the imagination and ritual of the Salvadoran state, so the Eucharist is the imagination and ritual of the church (Cavanaugh, *Torture and Eucharist*, 229). I can still feel the chills. Walking this holy ground, following in the footsteps of martyrs, made me think of the apostles and their contact with Jesus. I was overwhelmed by the sacred.

That's the context; now let me turn to some lessons learned and the potential I see for American Catholics and for our own work here in Camden. For this analysis and reflection, I concentrate on the pastoral vision of Archbishop Romero.

ROMERO: LESSONS FROM A PASTOR AND PROPHET

My reflections on my journey were greatly aided by reading *Archbishop Oscar Romero: A Shepherd's Diary*. This complete diary had the effect of a cold, hard reality check. It helped me to understand better Romero's struggle with the violence, oppression, and poverty that his people faced. The eye-opener was to see how this bishop's life, day in, day out, was packed tight with the mundane—meetings, negotiations, and personal and institutional conflicts—but he never lost sight of the need to incarnate in his pastoral vision the presence of Christ and the workings of the Spirit in the community. He never lost sight of the church's fundamental option for the poor. Most important, he never forgot that "in the Eucharist the poor are invited to come and to feast in the Kingdom. The Eucharist must not be a scandal to the poor" (Cavanaugh, *Torture and Eucharist*, 263). That is what I brought back with me to Camden.

But let's turn first to his life. As priest and bishop, Romero was not a boat rocker. When he was chosen archbishop of San Salvador in 1977, his conservative counterpart bishops breathed a sigh of relief. His bookish demeanor bode well for the defenders of the status quo. The many priests and lay leaders who were working for social change and defense of the poor were disappointed. He was the perfect "center-traditional" selection. But just as Romero became archbishop, a new president took office. Ironically, his name was also Romero—but that Romero had no intention of defending the poor. Within a few days, thousands of people protested in San Salvador's Plaza Libertad. Army troops opened fire killing many and sending the poor running to the only place of relative safety—the church.

I notice that in Romero's diary, he was constantly faced with the problem that his cathedral was being occupied by a variety of groups representing the poor. He understood well the need of the "popular" organizations to have a place to organize and get protection. But as a pastor, he had to face the practical issue of how to accommodate the faithful in their liturgical life. The archbishop-pastor is indeed practical. On Sunday, February 24, 1980, his diary entry begins,

> We still held mass at the basilica, even though the Cathedral is no longer occupied, it is still very dirty and smells bad . . . but we understand that our people need to be able to find refuge in the Church, given a horrible situation of oppression . . . we are living. (quoted in Hodgson, *A Shepherd's Diary*, 501)

The tragic events of torture and murder escalated within days of Romero's installation as archbishop. His friend, Fr. Rutilio Grande, a Jesuit, was shot at the wheel of his car, along with an old man and a sixteen-year-old boy. Grande was pastor in Aguilares, where the workers of the cotton and sugarcane fields lived in poverty. For the new archbishop, the murder was a moment of truth. As he prayed over his dead friend, he was faced with conversion—a New Testament–style *metanoia*. He knew that he would have to choose sides.

I realize that there is considerable debate as to how much of a radical conversion can be found in Romero after he became archbishop. Some claim to trace more continuity than others. I will not try to answer that question but only indicate that Romero clearly became the voice of the poor but always speaking with them and not just for them. Working with his pastoral team and Jesuit scholars at the university, he set in motion a church that stood against repression and for human and civil rights. His weekly broadcast homilies, which integrated the weekly news with scriptural and theological reflection, became the hallmark of his pastoral vision and, eventually, the only hope for the poor and disenfranchised.

Nonetheless, the terror increased with each passing day. The army and private death squads burned villages, desecrated churches, and tortured and executed priests, nuns, and lay leaders. The killers proudly distributed handbills that said, "Be a patriot, kill a priest."

The shy but courageous pastor refused to be intimidated. However, he began to live his life in the shadow of death. His pastoral approach, relating everyday events to theological reflection, more and more confronted the power structures—governmental, military and economic. His words— as theologian Jon Sobrino, SJ, tells us—still send "chills up spines today":

> I rejoice, brothers and sisters, that our church is persecuted precisely for its preferential option for the poor . . . How sad it would be, in a country where such horrible murders are being committed, if there were no priests among the victims! A murdered priest is a testimonial of a church incarnate in the problems of the people. . . . A church that suffers no persecution, but enjoys the privileges and support of the powers of the world—that church has good reason to be afraid! But that church is not the true church of Jesus Christ. (quoted in Sobrino, *Archbishop Romero*, 38)

Romero gradually realized that the church could no longer stand with the status quo as it had throughout the history of Latin America. While not becoming political, in a partisan way, the church's pastoral action had to engage the political and economic realities of the country. As archbishop, he had to walk a fine line. He vehemently condemned all violence, whether of the Left or Right, but he knew that the poor of El Salvador were victims of the government and the military, both of which had the support of U.S. economic and military power. A sad note, during the troubled times, was that Romero could not rely on most of his fellow bishops for support. Some of them were closely identified with the government, ruling class, or military. Moreover, Salvadoran and

American pressure contributed to Vatican suspicions about the archbishop's stance.

Indeed, Romero had enemies, but he also had friends. In November 1978, the British Parliament nominated him for the Nobel Peace Prize. The award eventually went to Mother Theresa, but other international groups honored his efforts for peace. In February 1980, not long before his death, the University of Louvain honored Romero with an honorary doctorate. This allowed him a platform to lay out his pastoral vision. At the same time, he was able to go to Rome to plead his case and that of his people to Pope John Paul II. On his return home, he wrote to President Carter, asking him not to send military aid to the Salvadoran government. On February 18, 1980, his diary refers to the war on the poor of El Salvador and to the heartburn caused by his letter—not only in San Salvador but also in Washington and Rome:

> This kind of war purports to do away not only with the people directly responsible but also with their families who, according to this theory, are totally poisoned by these terrorist concepts and must be eliminated. The danger, then, is great, and the letter is to ask the President of the United States not to send military aid that would mean great injury to our people because it would mean the destruction of many lives (quoted in Hodgson, *A Shepherd's Diary*, 493).

By now Romero was a serious threat and a marked man. Nonetheless, he stuck to his pastoral vision. He and his advisors tried to carefully analyze the political, social, and economic context and bring to bear on that context the gospel message and values. This was the methodological essence of his pastoral approach in a highly politicized atmosphere. Nonetheless, Romero's own personal humility constantly emerges in his deliberations, his organizing, and his planning. He even admits to "defects" in his character and, in a most positive way, his dependence on his people and advisors: "We cannot take the risk of staying on the sidelines at such a historic time. But we must be sure that our presence has a true ecclesial identity" (quoted in Hodgson, *A Shepherd's Diary*, 506–7).

That he was able to maintain such balance amid bitter divisions is a tribute to his humility, his dedication to the church, and his deep prayer life. Indeed, when reflecting on Romero's pastoral life and leadership, it gradually becomes clear that time was running out and that death was drawing near. He seems to have lived his last weeks and even months in the shadow of the paschal mystery. He stated, "If I am killed, I will rise again in the people of El Salvador. If God accepts the sacrifice of my life, let my blood be a seed of freedom. . . . Let my death be for the liberation of my people, as a witness of hope in the future."

On March 23, 1980, he preached his last homily in the cathedral. He ended with a plea to the soldiers:

> Brothers, you are part of our people. You are killing your brothers and sisters. No soldier is obliged to obey an order that is contrary to the law of God. . . . In the name of God and in the name of this suffering people, whose screams and cries mount to heaven, and daily grow louder, I beg you, I entreat you, I order you in the name of God: Stop the repression! (quoted in Sobrino, *Archbishop Romero*, 89)

This was the death knell. This was treason. On the next day, Monday, March 24, 1980, Romero went to the chapel at Divine Providence Hospital to celebrate Mass for the mother of a friend. The Mass began at six in the evening. The archbishop's short homily praised the faith of his friend's mother and her concern for the poor and oppressed. He concluded,

> The holy mass, now, this Eucharist, is just such an act of faith. . . . May this body immolated and this blood sacrificed for humans nourish us also, so that we may give our body and blood to suffering and to pain—like Christ, not for self, but to bring about justice and peace for our people. Let us join together, then, intimately in faith and hope at this moment of prayer for Doña Sarita and ourselves (quoted in Hennelly, *Liberation Theology*, 306).

At this moment, a gunman, who had entered the chapel hallway, fired one shot through the archbishop's heart. He died within moments at a nearby emergency room. The gunman escaped, and it took thirteen years before an investigative commission would trace responsibility to a high-ranking government official. More than 100,000 people came to the funeral— many poor *campesinos* who traveled miles by bus or on foot. They never forgot their "Saint Romero." Indeed, Romero—a strong believer in Christ's resurrection and in all of our resurrections—lives on in the lives of his people. In him, Salvadorans had seen a leader who heard the cry of the oppressed, who pleaded for structural changes, and who encouraged the poor to organize. He judged any political solution by the unique criteria of the good of the poor: "Archbishop Romero's great love was shown not only in his defense of the poor. It was also shown in his identification with them, to the very cross" (Sobrino, *Archbishop Romero*, 208).

CONCLUSIONS AND APPLICATIONS

My pilgrimage helped me to grasp better the need to radicalize the gospel in my own ministry and in our work here in Camden. I realize that we have already tried to do that. However, stepping outside of one's own environment and one's own problems offers a fresh perspective. It broadens our vision. That's what this trip did for me. I realized—in a much clearer fashion—what the liberation theologians and Romero had long said: theological reflection and church life should start with human experience, the local community, the people—especially, the poor and marginal in our society. I understand better now what Gustavo Gutiérrez meant when he said that theology begins with reflection on everyday life: "Christian reflection on Christian praxis." That is not only true for San Salvador; it is equally true for Camden, Trenton, or Washington, D.C.

Archbishop Romero wanted the church to be neither a museum piece nor a political organization. But he knew that to be the true continuation of the Incarnation, the church had to take up the challenge of justice in all of its political, social, and economic dimensions. His pastoral vision encompassed analysis of current reality from the perspective of the poor, theological reflection on that reality, a keen sense of hope in the future, and support for organization and action by the faithful. That approach is applicable everywhere.

At this beginning of the new millennium, we should all be helping the church to become more of a transnational, global actor. We need to overcome and break down our petty barriers—national, ethnic, racial, and economic. Romero's approach to learning, leadership, liturgy, and lay leadership can help us all to be more "Catholic." What a model he was for this global age. His witness, his vision, presents us with a dual challenge: the challenge to be truly Catholic and the challenge to question even, at times, the direction of the church. It is that "creative fidelity" that was his gift.

Preparing his homily with the newspaper in one hand and the Bible in the other illustrates the core of his pastoral vision and practice. He forged that practice in dialogue with the poor and oppressed: "With this people, it is not difficult to be a good Shepard" (quoted in Sobrino, *Archbishop Romero*, 13).

Romero and the other martyrs are helping me to be a better pastor. They also helped me to broaden my horizons and to see that indeed Camden's problems of housing, education, crime, and joblessness relate to those of the suffering and poor worldwide. Reading the "signs of the times" in the sense of Vatican II is for all of us now a global thing. We need to work for the poor right here in New Jersey, but we also need to raise consciousness and work for the poor around the world. For example, we should be aware of the implications of U.S. government support for the years of killing and oppression in Central America. It was our tax dollars that paid for the slaughter.

Theological reflection on current reality articulates our commitment to justice and to the poor. That commitment is not something added on to our faith, nor is it something nice to do. It is of the essence of our Catholic faith. The footsteps of the martyrs took me back to the 1971 Synod of Bishops, *Justice in the World:*

> Action on behalf of justice and participation in the transformation of the world fully appear to us as a constitutive dimension of the preaching of the Gospel, or in other words, of the Church's mission for the redemption of the human race and its liberation from every oppressive situation. (no. 6)

The synod's vision is Romero's vision. Indeed, it is the Catholic pastoral vision. I hope that the Romero Center will become a focal point for reflection on that vision and that "constitutive dimension" of the gospel, raising awareness around faith and justice issues in Camden, in our country, and in our world.

DISCUSSION QUESTIONS

1. Discuss the qualities that you think made Romero such a dedicated pastor and leader. How might his model of leadership help us in the United States?
2. What did the "option for the poor" mean for Romero? Why do you think so much violence and hatred were directed toward priests in Central America?
3. Romero always sought to "think with the church." What does that mean? Do you think that Archbishop Romero should be canonized? Why? Why not?

RESOURCES AND FURTHER STUDY

Brackley, Dean. *Divine Revolution: Salvation and Liberation in Catholic Thought.* Maryknoll, N.Y.: Orbis Books, 1996.

Brockman, James. *Romero: A Life.* Maryknoll, N.Y.: Orbis Books, 1989.

Cavanaugh, William T. *Torture and Eucharist: Theology, Politics, and the Body of Christ.* London: Blackwell, 1998.

Enemies of War. Video. Produced and directed by Esther Cassidy. Co-directed by Rob Kuhns. Co-produced by Cassidy/Kuhns Productions and SCETV. Washington, D.C.: Catholic Communication Campaign, 1999.

Hennelly, Alfred T., ed. *Liberation Theology: A Documentary History.* Maryknoll, N.Y.: Orbis Books, 1990.

Henriot, Peter J., Edward P. Deberi, and Michael J. Schultheis. *Catholic Social Teaching: Our Best Kept Secret*. Maryknoll, N.Y.: Orbis Books, 1992.

Hodgson, Irene B., trans. ed. *Archbishop Oscar Romero: A Shepherd's Diary*. Cincinnati, Ohio: St. Anthony Messenger, 1986.

Sobrino, Jon. *Archbishop Romero: Memories and Reflections*. Maryknoll, N.Y.: Orbis Books, 1990.

Synod of Bishops. *Justice in the World*. Washington, D.C.: United States Catholic Conference, 1971.

2

The Eucharist and Social Justice

John P. Hogan

The horrific events of September 11, 2001, have brought death much closer to us all. But ideally, it has also brought life, faith, family, and community closer to us as well. One grace that arises out of the ashes might be to make us more aware of the children, families, and communities that live life everyday close to death—the death of poverty, the death of drugs, the death of crime.

Being from Brooklyn and from a family of cops, firefighters, and World Trade Center types, I have two images from September 11 that have really stayed with me. The first is from the *New York Times* article on the two lines of traffic in the towers—one running down the stairs (usually, financial management types) and the other running up the stairs (usually, firefighters). Both took heavy losses; many from both lines died. In a bizarre tale of smoke, steel, and fire, lots of very different kinds of people were thrown together. They were one body, sacrificed together.

A second image that has stayed with me is that of the firefighters carrying their beloved but dead chaplain Father Mychal Judge. There is a story that has grown up around that image—perhaps apocryphal—that the young firefighter who first found the priest's dead body was asked by a reporter what he felt and did. The fireman responded, "I did the only thing I could. I closed his eyes and forgave him his sins, just like Father Mike had done for so many of us."

I can't vouch for the veracity of that story, but it is a beautiful depiction of all of us being thrown together in crisis and being reflective of and responsible for one another, another image of sharing, thanking, and forgiving—that's a Eucharistic image.

In this chapter, I follow Archbishop Romero's example and present some reflections on the connection between the commitment to social justice and the church's liturgy—the Eucharist. It's a connection that, unfortunately, has too often been forgotten. Let us begin with that graphic scene from the film *Romero*:

> A bishop stands at the altar in a simple chapel, celebrating Mass in the company of a few sisters. He blesses and elevates the host and then blesses and raises the cup. As he does so, a single shot rings out. The bishop falls, the blood of Christ mingling with the blood of the bishop (Hill, "Poured Out for You," 414).

As Rowena Hill points out, the film version takes considerable artistic license with the life of Oscar Romero, but that license is indeed warranted: "*Romero* is . . . a vivid demonstration of the way in which the commitment of the church to justice and peace is related to worship and sacramental life." In her excellent commentary on the film, Hill continues,

> This insight—the intricate connection between the commitment to social justice and the church's liturgy—is one that the church itself has frequently (if not consistently) failed to make. In papal encyclicals, for instance, which address questions of social justice (from *Rerum Novarum* to *Centesimus Annus*), liturgy and the sacraments are conspicuous by their absence. The defense of human dignity and freedom seems to be an aspect of the church quite distinct from what it does in worship. Yet the makers of *Romero* seem to suggest that, on the contrary, the connection between liturgy and justice is self-evident. Their Bishop Romero, in speaking and acting for justice, simply lives out what is shown forth in worship. To behave differently would make nonsense of the liturgy of which he is the chief celebrant (415).

My own perspective comes from the debate that has been crystallizing around the very issue that Hill sees as being central to the life of Archbishop Romero—the linkage between Eucharist and justice. My steps in pursuit of that linkage were quickened by Kathleen Hughes's pointed question "When Jesus said, 'Do this in memory of me,' what was the *this* he had in mind?" John Coleman, SJ, recently reminded us that social justice finds its roots in and is fed by the Eucharistic imagination. He adds, "How then have we so lost our way that such claims can seem provocative?" ("How the Eucharist," 5). Eucharist is the essence of Christian praxis, the fulfillment of baptism, a thankful yes to Jesus's life, death, and resurrection that incorporates us as a spirited community to do as he did—seek and build the Kingdom of God. Indeed, this understanding runs throughout our tradition. What went wrong? How did we come to so privatize Eucharist and separate it from community and concern for justice?

Could it be that we have let a too individualistic and therapeutic emphasis on "real presence" obscure the deeper meaning of Christ's presence and action in us as a community of believers? St. Augustine said, "We eat the body of Christ to become the body of Christ" (Himes, *Doing the Truth in Love*, 118). What in the world might that mean in the twenty-first century? What should it mean for the people of Camden, of Philadelphia, indeed, for Christians everywhere?

How should we relate our Sunday liturgy to the quest for justice? To cite here just one example, when and how might Eucharist—the sharing of the body and blood of Christ—call us to be open to the positive potential of economic growth and development? On the other hand, when and how might Eucharist be a real symbol of a needed resistance to growth and development that desecrates the environment and discards human beings as "collateral damage" of economic "progress"? How might Eucharist provide the theological basis for Catholic social teaching on solidarity, subsidiarity, and the option for the poor? How might it be coupled with a discernment process that rests on the Eucharistic imagination, builds community, and takes action on behalf of justice?

With these kinds of questions in mind, I will try to get to the "this" in Jesus's mandate. First, I concentrate mainly on St. Paul's treatment of Eucharist in 1 Corinthians as a basis for social justice and solidarity. Second, I briefly present some examples of justice issues, both global and local, with implications for Eucharist. And third, I sketch some ideas for a critical Eucharistic discernment process; a short conclusion ends these reflections.

ST. PAUL: DISCERNING THE BODY OF CHRIST

The New Testament is replete with stories of invitations to homes and fellowship meals. There were lots of dinner parties. At these affairs, Jesus can be heard constantly reminding his friends to be thankful. But he also used such occasions to reach out to hookers and hustlers. One thing jumps out: participants in the dinners and picnics are all treated as equals; all receive the same meal. There was no first class.

Jesus's last meeting with his disciples was also a meal of thanksgiving and blessing that stretched back to earlier covenants and particularly to the Passover. However, this meal was special. This time, Jesus changed the traditional blessing. Before he broke the bread, he said, "This is my body." In effect, he was saying that "not only is this bread a reminder of the Passover bread that our ancestors ate, but this bread is also me." He announced that "this wine was his blood, the blood of the new covenant." The participants in the new covenant became blood relatives, not only of Jesus, but also of one another, and with that comes responsibility for the extended family. The new covenant has some demanding terms. In John's Gospel, a foreshadowing of those terms is laid out when the master washes the feet of his disciples. He reverses the whole social order and scandalizes his closest followers— especially, Peter—a true Romero image.

Let me turn now to St. Paul's treatment of the Eucharistic celebration in 1 Corinthians 11:17–34. For this section, I am indebted to John Haughey, SJ, who does an excellent job of unpacking that text. The lessons to be learned from Paul clearly apply to our task. Here, Paul is seeking to get to the root of the insensitive behavior of the Corinthians. He aims for the deeper meaning of "real presence" as the body of Christ identified with the community. "Defective perception of the mystery of the Lord's presence in the community led to defective internalization, and, in turn, to [defective] social behavior" (Haughey, "Eucharist at Corinth," 108–9). The Corinthians, in spite of their belief in the real presence, did not get it. Their understanding was very much tied up with an "individuated Christ." There was little or no grasp of "being members of one another in a whole which is his sacred presence." Paul's concern gets behind interpersonal behavior as well as racial, national, economic, ideological, and social divisions. Maybe, we still suffer from the Corinthian myopia.

Had the Corinthians understood Eucharist as the presence that unites members in the body and creates a single entity, they would have realized how sacrilegious their behavior toward one another was. We can only imagine what it might have been toward non-Christians. "A nascent gnosticism was developing in Corinth which had some portion of the community of believers verticalizing and spiritualizing their faith in Christ" (Haughey, "Eucharist at Corinth," 113). This manifested itself both in inflated egos and in a lack of concern for the less educated, the stranger, the poor, and the slave. Then as now, Jesus's humanity seems to have posed more of a problem than did his divinity. Paul is reminding the community that Jesus said that he would be there in the poor, the prisoner, and the foreigner but he is also raising the trinitarian dimension "that they all may be one in us" (John 17:21).

If the aforementioned textual reasoning is accurate, as it appears to be, Jesus's mandate "to do this in memory of me" would then mean, "Do this again and again by remembering me at your table fellowship. But you remember me if you know my presence with you is through one another whom I am fashioning into so many members of my own body." In Paul's view, the private individual possession of Christ comes at no cost and is selfish. Rather, he understood Eucharist as participation in a concrete, communal way. Haughey refers to this as "relational wholeness," which makes us Christ's body and members of one another: "The knitting together of individuals would be their redemption and at the same time would be the beginning of the recapitulation of all systems in Christ" (Haughey, "Eucharist at Corinth," 120–23).

This understanding of Eucharist offers intriguing food for thought for realizing Christ's presence on a global scale and in the Christian quest for justice. Paul sees the concrete working out of real presence in a community of people who are open and who identify not with the few, the like-believers, but with all—with Christ himself in the whole body. But there is great movement and freedom within that body, precisely because "they were Christ's body." To grasp what Paul seems to be saying is startling. Together, we are Christ. We are one with the "social flesh" of the word of God. Christ's death and resurrection can now become the determinants of our lives. If we are truly members of his body, he is now us (Haughey, "Eucharist at Corinth," 125–27).

JUSTICE AND THE BODY OF CHRIST

Clearly, this approach to Eucharistic presence puts theological flesh on the theoretical bones of Catholic social teaching—solidarity, subsidiarity, and the option for the poor. It provides the "body"—head, hands, and feet—for the church as a transnational, global actor for justice. It is a much more "real" presence than a privatized, individuated Jesus in a host. If we can realize this "relational wholeness," we can be a lot more effective in terms of socioeconomic policy and social justice. We cannot claim to be Catholic and Christian, the body of Christ, and support structures and systems that keep people poor and powerless.

Unfortunately, if we examine our Eucharistic record, we too often come up wanting. Indeed, some situations might indicate a failure of Eucharist. One need only think of Chile under Pinochet, Central America, during the 1970s and 1980s; Rwanda, before and during the genocide; Northern Ireland; and the Balkans. All were situations where Eucharist was celebrated daily but became symbolic of division and exclusion rather than unity and inclusion. How many opportunities for reconciliation and forgiveness were missed? And, perhaps, when we look at our own situation of economic and racial segregation, the plight of our cities, tax structures, and the global neglect of the poor the issue comes much closer to home. Paul's concerns are both local and global. He warns the Corinthians and us, "Examine yourself, and only then eat of the bread and drink of the cup. For all who eat and drink without discerning the body, eat and drink judgment against themselves" (1 Corinthians 11:28–31). If not properly discerned, Eucharist can be dangerous to our health.

Two insights for our contemporary situation emerge from St. Paul's warning to the Corinthians. The first is a renewed sense that his embodied

Eucharist is needed to infuse a global Catholicism incorporated in each local community and committed to social justice. "Not in my backyard" has no place in the body of Christ. We are all called to work toward that evasive but always faintly present Kingdom of God. That is the meaning of the "this."

Second, the paschal mystery provides Christians with a "master narrative" in an epoch without master narratives (Schreiter, *The New Catholicity*, 60). Every person, every community, needs a story, a guide to life. The Eucharist, our celebration of the passion, death, and resurrection of Jesus—like the struggles of Archbishop Romero and the struggles of the people of Camden—brims with ironies of betrayal, denial, broken promises, and abandonment. Like Peter, we have all heard the cock crow, but at least we've heard it. Most important, the story, as we know, ends in great surprise. Death is overturned by new life. Resurrection trumps death.

We reenact our master narrative, our story, every Sunday. But without a broader understanding of the central act of Christian worship, we run the risk of aiding and abetting the growing separation of the rich and poor—the church of the rich and the church of the poor. Indeed, Eucharist is where Catholics are educated in their faith.

CRITICAL DISCERNMENT AND RELATIONAL WHOLENESS

Let me move briefly to the educational potential of the Eucharist—to the process of critical discernment and how to get to the "relational wholeness" mentioned earlier. I suggest a few practical steps for relating Eucharist to social justice. The kind of discernment process I propose allows us, even demands of us, that we bring together in the Eucharist the three paths of conversion, communion, and solidarity with the poor, which Pope John Paul II called us to in *Ecclesia in America*. In a very real sense, being part of the body of Christ challenges us to identify ourselves with the poor of Camden and with the poor around the world. We all share the same Eucharistic master narrative, the same paschal mystery where life conquers death.

To cite just one example from Catholic social teaching, let us consider the principle of solidarity, a central theme of Pope John Paul II. The concept of solidarity needs to be more than a principle and an attractive slogan. Solidarity with the poor implies identification with the poor. For Catholic Christians, this is a Eucharistic question. As the *Catechism of the Catholic Church* tells us, "The Eucharist commits us to the poor" (no. 1397, 353). For solidarity to really reflect the ontological unity of humankind redeemed in Christ, our embodiment of him, and him in us, needs to be preached and reflected on during liturgy, emphasized in the prayer of the faithful, and discussed in communal discernment sessions. Such discernment should, at times at least, include honest, open, interreligious, and intercultural dialogue.

Eucharist means the real presence of Jesus both in the elements of bread and wine and in the body of believers. The majority of Catholics would probably agree with the former but scratch their heads at the latter. For most of us, Eucharist is an interior retreat—a "spiritual" thing. One corollary, as we have seen, is the virtual absence of liturgy and Eucharist from official Catholic social teaching, as well as the relatively recent separation of liturgy from social thought and action. Both of these developments are serious betrayals, not only of the liturgical movement, but also of the New Testament and patristic traditions, since they deny the Eucharist its rightful educational role.

So, how might we move toward a deeper and wider meaning of Eucharist as the body of Christ in the body of believers? I contend that an inductive, practical discernment process has to be built into our Eucharistic celebrations that brings out the communal, bodily nature of Eucharistic presence and relates that presence to justice issues in this global age. We need to begin with the experience of our own local community and then work out from there. How do we experience community? How do we experience justice or injustice? How do people around us or across town experience it? Put bluntly, do we even know any poor people? How and why does being the body of Christ call us to seek solidarity with them? Are we in need of conversion from our habits, our ways of life, our ways of thinking? How do we reflect on our own experience when we have pulled it together into a personal and communal story? How do we judge our experience, our situation, our story? Do we use the Gospels and Catholic social principles of solidarity, subsidiarity, and the option for the poor to inform our judgment? Do we need to change? Can we act on our judgment? What action should we take? What can we do about the situation?

Of course, the aforementioned is a shorthand version of Bernard Lonergan's method: experience, understanding, judgment, decision (action). It is not the only discernment process that can serve our purposes, but it is one that clearly maps the cognitive and hermeneutical process and has been put to excellent use in examining the theological implications of social justice issues at the Woodstock Theological Center in Washington, D.C.

This process is akin to the discernment to which Paul was calling the Corinthians, but it is broadened to our times and to global horizons. In the Eucharist, we "put on Christ" and relive his story and, in doing so, discover our own. This is what we are called to do at every Eucharist. Outcomes of the process might take many forms, global or local, from concern for Africa or Latin America to a commitment in solidarity for the renewal of cities such as Camden. Decisional actions might run the gamut from advocacy to volunteer efforts, to parish twinning, to support for the Catholic Campaign for Human Development or the Catholic Relief Services.

Such an approach will help us to realize with St. Paul that we should not individualize Eucharist too much, we should not spiritualize Eucharist too much, and we should not isolate Eucharist too much. Rather, an approach implemented within the context of Eucharistic presence as "relational wholeness" could ignite communities to take up some of the difficult socioeconomic challenges. The stock market, terrorism, urban blight, drugs and crime, immigration, racial/religious/ethnic conflict, unfair labor practices, and HIV/AIDS seem to define our globe. Distance no longer cleanses dividends. Drugs flow out of Camden while sewer waste flows in. Since, so far at least, most of us are the "winners," we need to understand our role as members of the body of Christ and our responsibilities to the so-called losers. That might be what Augustine meant by "we eat the body of Christ to become the body of Christ."

CONCLUSION

Being the body of Christ means that we cannot practice Eucharist without practicing ethics. Worship, witness, and work for justice are intimately linked. They form a trinity, and they help us get to the "this" in Jesus's mandate. In the words of Nathan Mitchell of the University of Notre Dame,

> We are called to be—to become—a church that isn't afraid to dream; a church that isn't afraid to become what it heals; a church that isn't afraid to die (because only if it faces death fearlessly can it be empowered to live); a church that doesn't fear the body or its fluids or its failures; a church that isn't afraid to fail; a church that isn't afraid to forgive—or to ask forgiveness; a church that isn't afraid of speaking truth to power ("Editorial," 48).

Archbishop Romero, in different but nonetheless fearless language, echoes the same sentiment: "If it is seditious to reveal to people their identity as the Body of Christ and to remind them of the implications of this fact, then the liturgy of the Church is indeed seditious . . . " (quoted in Hill, "Poured Out for You," 420–21).

I am convinced that for the overwhelming majority of Catholics, education to solidarity, subsidiarity and participation, and the option for the poor will not happen unless it takes place within the context of Eucharist. "The whole of Catholic praxis is training in sacramental vision" (Himes and Himes, *Fullness of Faith*, 113).

We live out the meaning of the "this" when we link the Eucharist and social justice. Being the Body of Christ dares us to become a "church that not only does Eucharist but is Eucharist": a body given over in sacrifice. The church in Camden is rising to that task; the rest of us should, too. Romero would be delighted if we did.

DISCUSSION QUESTIONS

1. Talk about the role that the Eucharist played in Romero's life. How was it a sign of his commitment to his people? (The film *Romero* is a good resource for reflection.)
2. Discuss how your parish faith community might "move toward a deeper and richer meaning of the Eucharist as the body of Christ in the body of believers"?
3. What are some ways in which your parish might more closely relate Eucharist and social justice issues?

RESOURCES AND FURTHER STUDY

Catechism of the Catholic Church. Libreria Editrice Vaticana (Vatican Publishing House); Mahwah, N.J.: Paulist Press, 1994.

Coleman, John A. "How the Eucharist Proclaims Social Justice, Part 1." *Church* (Winter 2000): 5–8.

———. "How the Eucharist Proclaims Social Justice, Part 2." *Church* (Spring 2001): 11–15.

Connor, James L. "Theological Reflection: Woodstock's Way of Working." *Woodstock Report* (December 1992): 3–7.

Haughey, John C. "Eucharist at Corinth: You Are the Christ." In *Above Every Name: The Lordship of Christ and Social Systems,* edited by Thomas E. Clark, 107–33. Ramsey, N.J.: Paulist Press, 1980.

Hill, Rowena. "Poured Out for You: Liturgy and Justice in the Life of Archbishop Romero." *Worship* 74 (September 2000): 414–32.

Himes, Michael J. *Doing the Truth in Love: Conversations about God, Relationships, and Service.* New York: Paulist Press, 1995.

Himes, Michael J., and Kenneth R. Himes. *Fullness of Faith: The Public Significance of Theology.* New York: Paulist Press, 1993.

Hogan, John P. "Ecclesia in America: Towards a Catechesis of Global Solidarity." *Living Light* 35 (Summer 1999): 16–27.

Hughes, Kathleen. *The Liturgy That Does Justice.* Video. Preaching the Just Word Series 4. Chicago: Liturgy Training, 1995.

Hughes, Kathleen, and Mark R. Francis, eds. *Living No Longer for Ourselves: Liturgy and Justice in the Nineties.* Collegeville, Minn.: Liturgical Press, 1991.

John Paul II. "Ecclesia in America." *Origins* 28 (February 4, 1999): 566–92.

Mitchell, Nathan. "Editorial—Preaching the Just Word." *Assembly* 26 (November 2000): 48.

Romero. Film. Directed by John Duigan. Pacific Palisades, Calif.: Paulist Pictures, 1989.

Schreiter, Robert J. *The New Catholicity: Theology between the Global and the Local.* Maryknoll, N.Y.: Orbis Books, 1997.

3

If You Want Peace, Work for Justice

Thomas J. Gumbleton

This chapter addresses those profound words of Pope Paul VI: "If you want peace, work for justice." These words are especially important in considering the legacy of Oscar Romero. We are reminded of the spirit with which he brought all of his energy to work for justice in El Salvador. It was a time of extraordinary violence and killing, a time of extreme injustice. I think the best way to capture, to get an understanding of his spirit, the spirit with which he struggled for justice, is to begin with his own words. Two weeks before his murder, he was interviewed by a reporter who asked him, "Why don't you leave this country? Your name is on the death list. You will be killed."

Oscar Romero was aware that his name was on that death list, but he told the reporter, "I don't believe in death without resurrection. So even if they kill me, I will rise again in the Salvadoran people." He was a man of profound faith. He went on to say to the reporter, "As a shepherd, I am obliged by divine mandate—by the law of God—I am obliged to give my life for those I love." Then, he immediately named those he loved: "First, . . . I give my life for those I love, for those who may be going to kill me." At the end of the interview, he told the reporter, "If, in fact, they kill me, you may tell them that I forgive them and bless them."

I have had the privilege many times to stand behind the altar in the small chapel in San Salvador where Archbishop Romero was shot to death. And as I stood at that altar, I thought about him. After he preached the homily, walked back over to the altar, and offered the bread and wine, the door in the back of the chapel opened up, and the assassin entered with his high-powered rifle. The archbishop would have looked up, I'm sure, and the distance was short enough that he would have looked right into the eyes of his killer. But it wouldn't have been a look of fear, because he wasn't afraid to die. It would have been a look of love, of forgiveness. Oscar Romero teaches us more than anything else about the transforming power of the love of Jesus, an active love that we sometimes call *nonviolence*.

The only acceptable way, the only genuine way, to bring about justice in our world is through love. It will never be done through violence, through power, through coercion. It will never be done with the force of arms. We are not going to bring justice to Iraq by waging war. The only way to bring justice into our world is through acts of love—the way of Jesus Christ, the way of Oscar Romero.

We live in a world where it is important for us to be aware of how necessary the work of justice is because we live in a world where injustice is prevalent. We live in a world where 20 percent of the people, those living in the United States, Europe, and Japan, use 87 percent of the world's wealth and resources. In comparison, 20 percent of the world's people have only 1.7 percent of the world's wealth and resources. The bottom 20 percent live in extreme poverty, or what we have come to call *absolute poverty*. The remaining 60 percent of the world's people live in a situation that is more or less poor.

Absolute poverty, unless you have directly experienced it, is almost impossible to comprehend. Yet 20 percent of the world's people try to survive on a dollar or less a day. Robert McNamara was head of the World Bank when he began to travel to parts of the world where people lived in absolute poverty. He attempted to describe it and was overwhelmed by his experience. I remember hearing him speak about it, with tears in his eyes, as a situation where people barely survive on the margins of human life in a situation that is so degrading that you cannot even call it *human*.

A concrete image of what that means—one that is difficult to think about or to imagine but which perhaps will help us realize what absolute poverty really is—is something that I saw described in a newspaper at the time of Mother Teresa's death a few years ago. Mother Teresa worked in Calcutta, in one of the poorest slum areas of the world, and she died there. At her funeral, people from all over the world gathered; there were media from every part of the world. A reporter asked one of her volunteers from Japan, "How do you decide which person to pick up?" They would bring people close to death back to the center, knowing that they would not save these people's lives but simply give them some dignity—wash them, put them in a bed, minister to them, hold their hands as they were dying. "How do you decide which person to bring back?" The young volunteer responded, "When we see someone lying in the gutter, covered with their own excrement, we know that we must bring that person back." That's what it means to live in absolute poverty: lying in the gutter, covered with sewage and filth, covered with your own excrement. It's an ugly image, isn't it? But think about it: 1.2 billion people on this planet live in absolute poverty. When I think about that, I think about it almost as blasphemy because every person is made in the image and likeness of God and we allow this to happen to someone who has the dignity of being a son or daughter of God.

As we make ourselves aware of the extreme injustice that happens in our world, the most important thing for us to remember is to know that this does not happen by chance. This does not happen because people are lazy or because God wills it—certainly not. As Mother Teresa herself said, "God did not cause poverty. It is we humans who cause poverty in the world."

SINFUL SOCIAL STRUCTURES: POVERTY AND VIOLENCE

In El Salvador, there are many who were inspired by Oscar Romero and his constant struggle for justice for that tiny country, including the liberation theologians and the leaders of the base communities. And among the leaders of liberation theology were the Jesuits from the University of Central America in San Salvador. I am sure that most of us remember November 16, 1989, when six of those Jesuit theologians were murdered with two women who were their assistants. The day after that murder happened, the *Boston Globe* published a letter by Ignacio Ellacuria, SJ, one of the priests who were killed. He was the rector of the university, one of the formulators of liberation theology, and a leader in promoting justice. He wrote about the need for radical change and nonviolent revolution within El Salvador to make it a just society.

Father Ellacuria had written this letter three years before his death. In fact, it was published in the *Boston Globe* at that time and was republished on November 17, 1989. Father Ellacuria wrote the letter in response to Edward Sheehan, who was in the Public Affairs Office of the U.S. Embassy in El Salvador and who had written an article attacking the University of Central America and the Jesuits who ran the university as being too utopian, too destructive, too violent. Father Ellacuria knew that he had to respond to those charges because people might believe them and try to destroy the Jesuits and the work that they were doing.

In his response, he rejects any notion that the liberation theologians, the Jesuits, and those working for change in El Salvador under the leadership of Archbishop Romero were being destructive or violent. But he does say that, perhaps, Mr. Sheehan is closer to the truth when he says we are "utopian" because we are people of the Gospel, the Gospel of Jesus Christ, a Gospel that proclaims the reign of God and that calls us to transform our world into as close an image of the reign of God as possible. Some people would say that's utopian—the Gospel of Jesus Christ—the Gospel that calls us to proclaim God's reign of justice, God's reign of life, of peace, but it is our task to transform the world in which we live. And in doing so, an image of the reign of God becomes possible.

Father Ellacuria continues,

> It is not, then, that liberation theology, or Salvadoran Jesuits, are promoting violence. On the contrary, violence is what we are trying to overcome. But let us not deceive ourselves about where all this violence began.
>
> It started with what the church called institutionalized, legalized violence, whether in the form of economic exploitation, political domination, or abuse of military might. . . .
>
> In the case of El Salvador, the Jesuits here have condemned institutionalized and repressive violence, and we have done all that we could—including calling, even before the war began, for dialogue—to avoid and diminish revolutionary violence ("The Jesuit Vision," 19).

Violence starts with the structures of violence. The martyred Jesuit points out in the letter that when people begin to work against those structures of violence, those who have the system working in their favor will begin a counteractive violence of oppression. That is exactly what happened in El Salvador. People began to try to bring about revolutionary change, to build a more just society so that everyone had the possibility of participating in the goods and the blessings of that society. In response, the privileged few repressed the ones seeking change, so this violence of oppression became a violence of repression. As has happened in El Salvador, some of the oppressed came to the conclusion that the only way to bring about change is through the violence of revolution. Nonetheless, Father Ellacuria insists, "We struggle against that first violence, and we have worked against the violence of repression and we also struggle against revolutionary violence. We work to bring about negotiation, dialogue, reconciliation—we reject any kind of violence." He states, "To call our position violent is to make an erroneous judgment. We have endured a good deal during these years; one of us, Father Rutilio Grande, was murdered. The rest of us received an ultimatum 'Get out of the country or be killed.' We decided to stay. Since then our home and our university have been bombed fourteen times." And after that, of course, came the assassinations. The Jesuits were killed for working against structural violence, against the violence of repression, and against revolutionary violence.

Pope John Paul II is one who has made us acutely aware of injustice in the world—systemic and structural. He is the one who named that injustice "the structures of violence." And this is the term that is important for us to become familiar with because if we are going to work for justice in our world, then we must begin to understand how injustice happens. Why is it that we have a world in which 20 percent of its people live in absolute poverty and 60 percent in varying degrees of poverty while the remaining 20 percent enjoy 87 percent of the world's wealth? That doesn't happen because Americans and Europeans are smarter than everyone else. It doesn't happen because we work harder than the poor people on this planet. No, it happens because of the way that we have organized the international economic order—structures and systems.

Back in 1971, Pope Paul VI called a synod of bishops to discuss the question of justice in the world. He asked the bishops to try to grapple with this problem. Why is it that so many are so poor and so few are so rich? I have a sense that Pope Paul VI had strong feelings about this. This is why, first of all, he wrote an encyclical letter in 1967 called *On the Development of Peoples*. It is a passionate plea for the world's poor. Then in 1971, he called a synod of bishops to discuss the issue of justice in the world because he had gone to Calcutta and walked among the poor people lying in the gutter. It must have had a profound effect on him; he had never experienced anything like that before. I remember seeing a picture on the front page of the *New York Times* back at that time. It showed the pope standing there in the middle of a slum with mud splattered on his white cassock and a little child standing next to him, tugging at his side. It was a chilling and moving image.

In the 1971 synod, *Justice in the World*, the bishops stressed again and again that the faithful, particularly, the more wealthy and comfortable, simply do not see structural social injustice as sin. *Structural social injustice*: these are words that we should remember. The bishops emphasized that we do not see structural social injustice as sin, and so we feel neither obligation nor responsibility to do anything about it. They contrasted that with the Catholic emphasis on Sunday observance and the church's rules on sex and marriage. These tend to enter the Catholic consciousness profoundly as sin, but to live like Dives with Lazarus at the gate is not perceived as sin. In a powerful application of that parable, they suggested that the world in which we live is much like the New Testament story: the rich person, Dives, with Lazarus, the poor beggar at his door, neglected—no responsibility, no obligation. Dives does nothing. Our world is like that. We are Dives; Lazarus is at our gate. We do nothing. We see no responsibility for this situation nor feel any obligation to do anything about it. We must begin to understand that structural social injustice is sinful, that people do have a responsibility for that sin, and that we do have an obligation to do something about it.

Structural social injustice can be defined as a situation where some level of society—a city, a state, a nation, a community of nations, or the

international community—is organized in such a way that it works to
the detriment of individuals or groups within that society. That is what
we mean by *structural social injustice.* You organize the society in such a
way that it works to the favor of some and the detriment of others, that
it destroys individuals or groups. A clear, easy example is seen through
the apartheid in South Africa. That whole nation was organized according to its constitution, which had deliberately been written by people
who understood what they were doing. They organized the nation in
such a way that the majority of the people—the blacks and the people of
color—were deprived of any economic or political rights. They were
treated with brutality and violence, deprived of their dignity as human
beings. The whole nation was deliberately organized to make that happen. And the result was violence against the majority of the people. It
didn't happen by accident, of course; it didn't happen because the black
people were lazy. It happened because those in power structured the society that way.

A similar thing has happened in the international order in regard to the
global economy. We have organized it in such a way that the wealth of the
world moves from the poor to the rich. In 1960, the gap between the rich
and poor nations on our planet was thirty to one. And that decade was
called "the decade of development," when nations were going to try to
narrow that gap. At the end of the decade, the gap was even wider, and it
has continued to grow wider ever since. Today, it is about eighty-two to
one. The rich have gotten richer, and the poor have gotten poorer.

Make no mistake about it. There are structures that make that happen—
for example, trade agreements that cause the wealth to move from the
poor to the rich and the Third World debt problem that Pope John Paul
has spoken about time after time. Poor nations have debts even though
they have paid off the original loans received back in the 1970s many
times over, but they are further in debt now than they were back when
they got the original loan. There are structural adjustment programs imposed by the International Monetary Fund forcing nations to cut back on
their social programs to pay the debt service, therefore depriving their
own people of essential programs. Some of the poor nations of the world
spend more than half of their total national income on debt service when
the original loan has been paid back many times, but the debt goes on and
on and on and people get poorer and poorer and poorer.

There are many ways in which this structural social injustice can be
changed, but part of the problem, as noted before and as the bishops of
1971 synod suggested, is that "we who benefit from the system feel no responsibility for what is happening and have no sense that we have an obligation to do something about it." The bishops concluded and Pope Paul
VI concurred that

action on behalf of justice and participation in the transformation of the world fully appear to us as a constitutive dimension of the preaching of the Gospel, or in other words, of the Church's mission for the redemption of the human race and its liberation from every oppressive situation (Synod of Bishops, *Justice in the World*, no. 6).

If we are not doing action for justice, if we are not participating in trying to transform this world, trying to change it into as close an image of the reign of God as possible, then we cannot say that we are following the Gospel of Jesus. Action for justice and participation in the transformation of our world constitute preaching the Gospel—living the Gospel.

TODAY'S WORLD: A WORLD AT WAR

In the current context in which we live, where we are at war right now, I feel that it is necessary to say something about the ongoing bloody conflict in Iraq. On April 4, 1967, Dr. Martin Luther King Jr. gave a speech at Riverside Church in New York City, a year to the day before he was shot to death. He made this judgment: "Any nation that continues to spend more of its resources on arsenals of death and destruction than it does on programs of social uplift is a nation approaching spiritual death." It's a profound judgment, some may even say harsh. However, how many of us are aware of how much we are spending right now in this nation on our military budget? Almost $400 billion in the current year (2003), and that does not even count the cost of the war that we are engaged at present. Our government will not tell us how much this war is costing or how much it will cost to rebuild the nation of Iraq after we destroy it. But we continue to spend more and more on arsenals of death and destruction so that the head of our forces in the Persian Gulf, Gen. Tommy Franks, can say with pride, "We are going to attack Iraq with the largest force of destructive capability that has ever happened in human history."

We are spending extraordinary amounts of money to develop an arsenal of destruction, and we are carrying out that destruction. And I am convinced that it is leading us toward spiritual death. We cannot continue to do what we are doing as a nation and be alive with the spirit of Jesus; it is impossible. As the noted biblical scholar John L. McKenzie, SJ, points out, "if we don't know from the New Testament that Christ totally rejects violence, then we can know nothing of his person or message. It is the clearest of his teachings." Yet, we continue to use the way of violence, thinking that it will somehow bring justice into our world.

Pope John Paul II never faltered in his condemnation of the wars in Iraq. At the beginning of the first Gulf War, he cried out, "Never again war, no, never again war," because war destroys the lives of innocent people, because it throws into upheaval the lives of those who do the killing. It leaves behind a trail of hatred and resentment that makes it all the more difficult to solve the very problems that provoked the war. So, we are on a path of death and destruction that will make it all the more difficult to resolve the problems of injustice that exist in our world. We must turn away from that path; we must change our thinking about how to bring justice into the world, how to bring peace into the world. Each of us must develop deep within our spirit a conviction and a commitment to work for justice as the way to bring peace and to reject war as a means toward peace. Only working for justice will lead to peace.

WHAT CAN I DO? WORK FOR JUSTICE

Some of us might wonder, "How can I know enough about justice and peace? How can I find out? What do I do? How do I act to bring about change? How can I change the structures of violence that exist in our world? How can I do anything? What can I do? Who am I?" Those are the types of questions that we often ask ourselves.

Whenever I raise those questions, I remind myself of a woman named Marta whom I met in El Salvador many years ago, a peasant woman who probably had no more than a few years of elementary school education. And yet, at the time, she was one of the leaders of her community. Her village was organized as a Christian-based community where the people came together, shared their goods, reflected on the scriptures, and determined how they were going to live. It was a cooperative. And because they were living this way, they were a threat to the economic system of the country, and so they were often persecuted. The army would come through, burn their crops, and kill their animals.

At the time, I was visiting the area with a delegation from North America. We sat and talked with this leadership group, the village council. One member of the group asked Marta, "Why don't you tell them what just happened to you?" And so she did. Only a couple of weeks before, the military had come through the village and abducted her, taking her for interrogation as a leader of the community. They wanted to find out from her the names of people in the community who had family members that had left and gone into the hills to join the revolutionary movement. The village itself was not armed. They were committed to nonviolent change. But some of the families clearly would have had family members who had decided that only revolution, violent revolution, would work. But if she gave the names of those families, they would be identified immediately as Marxists, as communists, and their names would go on the death list. Marta refused to betray her neighbors.

She said that the first few times they interrogated her, they just screamed at her, harassed her verbally. Then, she said, after a while, they began to beat her with their fists and the butts of their rifles. Finally, after one of the interrogation periods, they beat her and tore off all of her clothes. She said, "They did to me what they wanted." Of course, it was violent and humiliating. Then, they let her go. When she was telling us about this, I was amazed because I sensed in her a deep surrender, a peace. It was clear that she had forgiven those soldiers. It was exactly according to the teachings of Oscar Romero: to bless, to forgive those who killed him. She was working for change but through nonviolence, through acts of love. And it's always amazing when you meet someone who truly is filled with that spirit of Jesus—but it's also puzzling. I asked her the same question that the reporter asked Oscar Romero, "Why do you stay here?" Obviously, they can come back anytime. They said to her when they let her go, "We'll come back, and the next time we'll kill you." I repeated, "Why do you stay?" Her response was "For me to answer you, you have to understand what it's like in this country. We have a situation where so few have so much, and so many have so little. That's not right." Then she added, "We are going to change that." Marta is a model for all of us. We should look around at our world and come to understand, as did this woman who had little formal education, and say, "That's not right!"

Most importantly, what we need is the courage of Marta, who was ready, no matter what they did to her, to say, "I am going to stay here and change that." When enough of us look around at our world and find out what's wrong and come to understand that so many have so little and that so few have so much and when we come to the conviction of "That's not right!" then we will have the courage to say as she did: "We are going to change that." Then, we'll have a world where all of us will begin to work for justice.

And by working for justice, we will bring peace to our world because "if you want peace, you must work for justice."

DISCUSSION QUESTIONS

1. What does Bishop Gumbleton mean by "sinful social structures"? Can you think of examples of such structures in your community, your parish, your city, the world? How does social sin relate to personal sin?
2. Discuss what role you think the United States plays in issues of global poverty. What responsibility do Americans have? Can we do anything about it?

3. The church, especially, Pope John Paul II, strongly condemned the war in Iraq, yet American Catholics, for the most part, supported the war. Why do you think that was so?

NOTE

For information on peace justice issues, see http://www.paxchristiusa.org.

RESOURCES AND FURTHER STUDY

Allen, John L. "Pope's 'Answer to Rumsfeld' Pulls No Punches in Opposing War." *National Catholic Reporter*, February 14, 2003. http://www.natcath.com/NCR_Online/archives/021403/021403e.htm (accessed May 2, 2007).

Burke, Kevin. *The Ground Beneath the Cross: The Theology of Ignacio Ellacuria.* Washington, D.C.: Georgetown University Press, 2000.

Ellacuria, Ignacio. "The Jesuit Vision." *Boston Globe*, November 17, 1989, 19.

Gregory, Wilton D. "Letter to President Bush on Iraq." Open letter, United States Catholic Conference, Washington, D.C., September 13, 2002. www.usccb.org/sdwp/international/bush902.htm (accessed May 2, 2007).

John Paul II. *Ecclesia in America.* Washington, D.C.: United States Catholic Conference, 1999.

———. *The Social Concerns of the Church—Solicitudo Rei Socialis.* Washington, D.C.: United States Catholic Conference, 1988.

Paul VI. *The Development of Peoples—Populorum Progresio.* Washington, D.C.: United States Catholic Conference, 1967.

Pax Christi USA. "Statement on War against Iraq." Washington, D.C., December 10, 2002. www.paxchristiusa.org/news_events_more.asp?id=317 (accessed May 2, 2007).

Romero, Oscar. *Voice of the Voiceless: The Four Pastoral Letters and Other Statements* With introductory essays by Jon Sobrino and Ignacio Martin-Baró. Maryknoll, N.Y.: Orbis Books, 1985.

Sobrino, Jon. *Christ the Liberator: A View from the Victims.* Maryknoll, N.Y.: Orbis Books, 2001.

Synod of Bishops. *Justice in the World.* Washington, D.C.: United States Catholic Conference, 1971.

U.S. Bishops. *The Challenge of Peace: God's Promise and Our Response.* Washington, D.C.: United States Catholic Conference, 1983.

———. *Economic Justice for All: Catholic Social Teaching and the U.S. Economy.* Washington, D.C.: United States Catholic Conference, 1986.

4

Liberation Theology for the Twenty-First Century

Gustavo Gutiérrez

L et me begin by recalling the profound witness of that committed priest and martyr Archbishop Romero. My last contact with Bishop Romero was by phone some weeks before his assassination. I called him to simply say hello and share some news. I ended our friendly conversation with a naïve expression. I said, "*Monseñor*, I need to go. Take care of yourself." And, after a short silence—for me, it was a long silence—he said, "Gustavo, in order to take care of myself, I would need to leave my country." He was sure—we were all sure—about the great likelihood that he would be killed. But he was conscious that his duty as a Christian and a pastor was to be with his people.

Liberation theology is a theology that speaks to and from the preferential option for the poor. If it were possible to quantify qualitative things, I would say that the preferential option for the poor forms 90 percent of liberation theology. This theology arises from the intention and goal to take seriously the challenge coming from poverty, the challenge to human consciousness, and, especially, the challenge to Christian consciousness. We begin with one conviction, that poverty is certainly a social and economic issue, but it is much more than that. I return to that focal conviction later.

Our context here is liberation theology in Latin American, only because I know this context so well. However, I am aware that liberation theology includes several other important trends and touches many geographical, social, and religious contexts. Nonetheless, this context of poverty in Latin America is a scandal of global proportions and is taking place on a predominately Christian continent. It is also a contradiction because poverty is contrary to the will of God. Our theology, the theology of liberation, arises from one question: "How can you tell a poor person that 'God loves you'?" That is how our theology begins. Certainly, it is possible to answer this question in a formal manner. God loves everyone. But, to be honest, to say to the poor person "God loves you" should not come easily, because the daily life of the poor seems like the negation of love. Nevertheless, our question must be, in what way and to what extent can we say not only that "God loves you" but even more than that. According to the Bible, the poor come first for God. This seems the height of irony because in reality the poor are last in our society.

That is our question. It is a practical question, a pastoral question. The deepest questions are always the pastoral questions. From pastoral questions, from practical questions, we get new theologies. From theological questions, we get new books. We need to deal with this gospel demand in the face of the grinding inhuman condition that is poverty. I present this question in three parts. First, I share some concerns about poverty and what we might call a new perception of poverty, although perhaps it is not so new. Second, I offer some reflections on the meaning of the preferential option for the poor. Third, I attempt to link the preferential option to the announcement of the Gospel.

NEW PERCEPTION OF POVERTY

From the very beginning of Christianity, two major lines of thought emerge about poverty. Both may be traced back to the Gospels and the witness of Jesus Christ. One centers on Jesus's sensitivity toward the poor and their suffering. For Jesus, the poor came first—children, women, prostitutes, and the sick. To be a follower of Jesus meant being open to the poor and being committed to doing something to alleviate their scandalous condition. The other line coming from the Gospel was that Jesus lived a poor life himself, and Christians, from the beginning, have understood that to be a disciple, they must in some way, to some extent, live a poor life, also. Both lines are true and evangelical. However, we need to understand these two perspectives from our own historical context and from our own life situations.

In some ways, we can find the first perspective in Luke's version of the beatitudes. "Blessed are the poor for the kingdom is yours" (6:20). The second perspective is closer to Matthew: "Blessed are the poor in spirit for theirs is the kingdom of heaven" (5:3). I think that both lines of thought—poverty as scandal and poverty as spirituality—are most helpful, but their meanings need to be clarified for our times.

Today—and, indeed, one could say, going back almost a century—there has been emerging a new perception of poverty. That perception comes from multiple sources. Let me mention a few. One concerns the complexity of poverty and the diversity of poverty. By this, I mean that poverty in the Bible and in our historical reality today is not only economic. Poverty is more than that. Certainly, the economic level is important, primary perhaps, but it is not the only dimension. There are others: cultural, racial, ethnic, and gender, to name a few. Poverty has these different dimensions, and in recent years, we have become more conscious of them. I want to be clear that when I speak about poverty and the poor, I am not thinking only of the economic level. Certainly, again, this aspect is most important, but still, it is only one aspect. Poverty was clearly the beginning of liberation theology, but we did not fully understand the complexity or diversity of that poverty.

Currently, the international agencies, the World Bank, for example, are speaking about the multidimensionality of poverty. The word is more complicated, but the idea is the same. Multidimensionality shows up in reports about poverty around the world. And for that reason, in the context of liberation theology, in spite of our limitations, the concept that we had of poverty many years ago still has value. We referred to the poor as nonpersons. This was meant, not in the philosophical sense, because clearly, every human being is a person, but rather in the social sense in that the poor were not accepted as persons in our society. They were invisible. They were without rights, without the recognition of their dignity.

We also called the poor "insignificant." You can be insignificant for several reasons: if you have no money, you are insignificant in our society; the color of your skin might be another reason to be considered insignificant; too often, simply being a woman means being insignificant. Insignificance, invisibility, lack of respect are what poor people have in common.

At the same time, these common complexes are diverse. A sense of nonperson can be bestowed by various prejudices: racial, gender, cultural, economic, and so on. The common characteristic for the poor person in our society is simply to feel and be irrelevant and insignificant.

I remember well back in 1969 hearing a statement from an American black church leader here in the United States. The opening sentence was "We must say we exist." That powerful statement is the cry of the poor. The poor Indians in my country, Peru, they do not exist. They are there physically, but they are invisible, irrelevant. Many years ago, an author named Manuel Scorza wrote a novel in which he describes the life of the poor invisible Peruvian Indian. He even called the book *Garabombo, the Invisible*. It is a sad story of an Indian going about his life, even going to a hospital for treatment, and being ignored. The central character in the novel captures well the sad plight of the Amerindian—his insignificance, his invisibility, his nonpersonhood. It is important for us when talking about poverty to be conscious of this kind of diversity, complexity, and multidimensionality.

Another point, relatively new as well, is that poverty today is a phenomenon of our global civilization. For centuries, we were more or less close to the poor as neighbors; the poor lived next to us in towns and in rural areas. But today, we have come to realize that poverty goes well beyond what we see; it is global. One might even say that it is universal. The majority of human beings in the world live in this condition that we call poverty.

This is important because if we look at books on spirituality, morals, or liturgy from the past, we immediately find that when writers address poverty and one's moral obligations to it, they speak only about how to help the poor directly, how to help the poor close by, how to help one's neighbor. Today, however, we need to recognize that our neighbors are both near and far. We must learn that "neighborhood" is the result of commitment. It is not a geographical question. It is now a global question.

I remember sometime ago speaking to a Swiss person before I had a chance to visit Switzerland. He was a good man, but he said to me, "You speak about poverty, but we have no poor people in Switzerland." Of course, that is not true when you take into account all the immigrants working there. But rather than argue with him, I said, "My friend, Switzerland is small. Go next door to France. Beyond Geneva, you will find many poor people." My response was a Christian one. If you say that in your country, you have no poor, then you have no responsibility. However, the Gospels never speak about national borders. Never.

Today, globalization is our new context. While national borders are diminishing in importance, the universality of poverty is increasing. Poverty is everywhere in the world, more and more inside rich countries, more and more within poor countries. The gap between the rich and the poor is getting wider—both between nations and between classes within nations. The human development reports of the United Nations over the last few years are clear about this. Poverty is driving a wedge between nations and people. Both rich and poor are being alienated by it and separated off from each other.

Nonetheless, what is even more important than the gap issue are questions concerning the origins of poverty and the place of poverty in our consciousness. These are more recent questions. For a long time, poverty was considered a fact, almost a fate. Some people were born into poverty; some people were born rich. Indeed, we even had a kind of uniform spirituality to deal with this stand. On one hand, there were two kinds of duties. The rich must be generous; the poor must be humble and accept help. It was all clear and, in a sense, easy. Most people considered their poverty not only as a fact, a natural fact, but also as the will of God. Imagine—the will of God was to create rich people and poor people! Until the middle of the twentieth century—recent times—we still had documents, official documents, even papal statements, speaking about poverty in this manner, as the "will of God."

Nonetheless, after many years of study and reflection, we have become more conscious of the historical causes of poverty. Now, we are coming to understand poverty as the result of the way that we have built and maintained our societies. It is a result of our mental categories—the way that we think and classify. I am especially thinking here of racial, cultural, and gender questions. If I think that one culture or race is superior and that others are inferior, the walls between the two just get higher and higher, as does aggression. The idea of separation becomes a hard mental category. We are conscious today of human reasons, human causes, for this plague we call poverty. They are economic, cultural, racial, social, and gender related. But at least we are coming to understand better, not everyone but many of us, that poverty is not destiny. It is a condition. It is not a misfortune. It is an injustice.

This is a relatively new approach to poverty and the poor. But it is a position often not understood or acknowledged, especially among the poor themselves. For many poor people—I have seen this in my neighborhood, in my parish—the view is "It is a shame, but I was born poor." And the idea of the will of God behind their condition is there all the time. Many poor people still think this way. But gradually, we and they are coming to realize that poverty has human causes. If we made poverty, we can eliminate poverty. However, we must realize that many of us, indeed, most of us, bear some responsibility in this question.

For the first time, perhaps, we have papal teaching that clearly expresses this point. John Paul II is the first pope to speak directly about the human causes of poverty and the social mechanisms that lead to poverty. He has done so often, and that is the thrust of his teaching on social, or structural, sin. When he was in Cuba, a communist country, he strongly emphasized that poverty has human causes. This has also been the general direction of the social sciences. In many ways, they have even been clearer than the Christian churches. This realization of the human causes of poverty, developing over the last fifty years, constitutes an important change in our manner of perceiving poverty.

Let me now turn to the last point of this first part. This concerns a more theological perspective. In the ultimate analysis, poverty means death—first, physical death, because poor people are dying of sicknesses that can often be easily cured by medical science today but not in poor countries. Second, in addition to this physical as well as economic death from poverty, there is a cultural side, a cultural death. Anthropologists say that "culture is life." When we despise a culture, a religion, a race, a gender, an ethnic group, we are killing persons—culturally speaking—belonging to that sector of humanity.

When the Dominican missionaries arrived in South America in the sixteenth century, they said, "The Indians are dying before their time." That is still true today. The poor worldwide are dying before their time, and they are dying a different kind of death. The death is still physical, but more so today, it is cultural.

Their dignity is denied, and they are not respected. This is a kind of death. If we see the question in this broader context, we can understand grinding poverty as being exactly contrary to the will of God because the gift of God is life. And that life includes the spiritual, material, and cultural. Poverty fights against this gift. It fights against the dignity of creation and the meaning of Resurrection.

Resurrection is the victory of life over death, while poverty means simply death. I think this is so because the root of poverty is the refusal to love. This theological reflection might be different from a sociological or psychological analysis. Nonetheless, we can say that at the root of poverty is injustice, which is the refusal to love—in other words, sin. Here, as elsewhere, the only sin is not to love. I realize that there are infinite variations of this sin. But in the end, sin is the refusal to love, and love is the core of what it means to be Christian. Thus, poverty is a challenge to Christian faith. It is a challenge to the announcement of the Gospel. And, therefore, it is a challenge to our reflection on our faith, our theology.

In this light, poverty is clearly not only a social issue, the personal concern of "social activists." To be concerned about poverty is not a special vocation to which some people are called. "He or she has a vocation to serve the poor." No, concern for the other, especially, the poor, is not a question of vocation. Vocation, rather, is the way that we are committed. But the commitment itself to fight this early and unjust death that is poverty is not the "vocation" of only the social activist. It is the task of every Christian. It is important to grasp this new perception of poverty, its causes and our role in the face of it, before moving on to the more specifically theological concerns surrounding the preferential option for the poor.

PREFERENTIAL OPTION FOR THE POOR

In this second part, I simply wish to discuss our three key terms: *preferential*, *option*, and *poor*. But, I want to reorder the words and start with *poor*.

Poor

A preferential option for the *poor* means the option for the *real poor*, or, if you prefer, the *material poor*. I do not like the expression, but I understand the need for it. It is the option for the *really poor* because the *poor in spirit*, as we will see, refers more appropriately to the followers of Jesus, the disciples. The first beatitude in Matthew concerns discipleship and is a focal theme in that Gospel. "Blessed are the poor in spirit" means "blessed are the disciples." To be poor in the spirit is to put our lives in the hands of God. One consequence of doing so is our detachment from material goods. But spiritual poverty is not primarily about the lack or denial of material goods. It is a consequence.

The meaning of *spiritual poverty*, or the synonymous evangelical expression *spiritual childhood*, can be understood through the metaphorical use of the expression. The ideal of "childhood" is that children are obedient (today, you might say, more or less obedient!). But it is or was the ideal. They put their lives in the hands of their mothers and fathers. This is where the notion of spiritual childhood comes from. Spiritual poverty is also a metaphor. As the really poor are dependent, the spiritual poor are dependent on God.

Our preferential option for the poor is a spirituality that includes the option for the really poor. It is not the option for the spiritually poor. The spiritually poor are holy persons. It should be the goal of all of us to be poor in spirit and to be holy persons. However, this is not the preferential option for the poor we are discussing. That option would be too easy—the poor in spirit are so few. Rather, it is clear from scripture and our tradition that this option is for the really poor—the millions and millions of poor suffering around the world.

Preferential

Let me move on to our second term, *preferential*, which in this context does not mean to moderate or weaken the option. That is a mistaken interpretation that has been made in some commentaries. Preference should be understood in relationship with universality. By that, I mean that God loves everyone—rich, middle class, poor, black, white—all of us. God's love is universal. At the same time, God clearly prefers the least, the abandoned, the insignificant person. The preference is a manifestation of the universality of God's love. There is no contradiction between universality and preference. However, there can be tension. There is the tension between prayer and action, also, but they are not contradictory. One is not the negation of the other. But tensions arise when trying to apply this universal love.

Nonetheless, for me, in the end, the most important person is the poor person. I'm sorry; it is not easy to hear, but that is our faith. For the God of Jesus Christ, every person—all of us—are relevant, important, and loved. But, we all need to make preferences. Otherwise, my love, our love, remains a vague universal—an abstraction. It is impossible to love every person in the same way. Some of you may know this in your experience as parents. Think of it: you love your children equally, but you need to treat them differently. You might have to protect the youngest because, otherwise, he or she might be treated unfairly by the bigger brothers and sisters. We all know the eternal question of children: "Mom, Dad, do you love my brother and sister more than me?" You also know the eternal answer: "No, I love you all equally."

In this context, we should know that preference does not mean to be against the rest. Rather, it is a way to underscore a need and work directly, for example, with the youngest or neediest in the family or with the sick person who needs our help most. The sick person becomes first for us, at least for a period of weeks, months, or years. However, as we know, it is not easy to keep universality and preference together. It is a challenge. Nevertheless, keeping them in tandem does not mean to moderate universality or to moderate preference. As I said earlier, that is a misunderstanding. I recognize the tension because I live with it daily and know how difficult it can be.

In the Gospel, it says, "Love your enemies." That is one of Jesus's major teachings. So, if you want to put the Gospel into practice, you must have at least one enemy! That is a humorous way of stating a serious point—we need to recognize the historical reality of adversity, both personal and social. In the midst of this human condition, one too often filled with adversity, how and where does love emerge? Moreover, this call to love our enemies reminds us of the universality of God's love. But why are we called to a preferential option—a preferential love for the poor?

Sometimes, when I speak about poverty outside of my country, people tell me, "I understand why you speak so strongly about poverty because you are a Latin American." My response is an old one, which I have repeated many times. "No, my friend, please don't jump to conclusions and understand me in this manner. My main reason for speaking about poverty is not because I am a Latin American—it is because I am a Christian." Many Latin Americans never speak about poverty. Frankly, the condition of being poor or from a poor country is sometimes not so helpful. Simply being close to poverty is not a sufficient reason to make one stand up against it.

To support our preferential option, we need to pose additional reasons. One such reason is certainly that of social analysis, which, as we have seen, allows us to understand the causes and patterns of poverty. This analysis is extremely helpful in preparing us to struggle alongside the poor and against poverty. However, even that social analysis is not the ultimate reason for the preferential option.

In the final analysis, the reason for the preferential option is that of human compassion. It is impossible to be committed to the poor without practicing compassion, in the true sense of the word. This sense of compassion—identifying with, feeling with the poor, so clearly shown to us in the life of Jesus Christ—is, as the Scholastic tradition would put it, both the first and the final reason for our option. I have heard people say that the reason for our compassion is that the poor are so generous. Often, this position comes from someone who has worked with the poor for a short time. After many years of working with the poor, my response is "not always and not all." I know many poor people who are most generous. I also know many who are not so generous. I have learned much from the poor and from their generosity. However, the poor are human, like the rest of us. They are bad persons and good persons. But the point is not the goodness or generosity of the poor. That is not the reason to be committed to them. It is not because the poor are good but because God is good. The ultimate reason for our commitment is theocentric.

Our preferential option is centered in God—not in the goodness of the poor. While many poor are good people and good Christians, that is not the reason for our compassion and option. The ultimate reason is that God is good and loves without fail. We need to understand this well. The love of God is gratuitous. In the Gospel of John, we are told that God loved us first. He loved us first—not as a result of anything we do, not after seeing if we are generous. First, in the beginning, before all else, was the gratuitous love of God. Christians often find it difficult to understand and accept this. Likewise, God loves the poor first, because the love of God is gratuitous. If the poor are good persons, better. But the more important question involves our understanding of God.

This understanding of God is most important, not only for the commitment to and with the poor, but for the whole of life. This gratuitousness is the great goal of every person. We seek to love gratuitously. And on the contrary, we are afraid of being loved because of our qualities. This fear comes because we know that we might one day lose those qualities. Gratuitousness is a central notion of the Gospel and the core of the spiritual poverty, or spiritual childhood, that I discussed earlier. This gratuitousness runs throughout the Bible and is especially important in the book of Job, who helps us to grasp the truth that justice alone does not have the final word about how we should speak of God. Only when we come to realize the gratuitousness of God's love do we enter into the real presence of the God of faith.

To pose God's gratuitous love as the reason for our preferential option and compassion for the poor might leave some with a lack of clarity. Gratuitousness is a mystery within the mystery of God. How can we understand this? It flies in the face of our experience. We love someone when he or she deserves our love. Otherwise, we back away. When we relate to the poor, if we relate to them, it is usually within a specific context. Our commitment is usually guided by charity and justice. It therefore has limits. However, the gratuity of God's love is limitless.

It is demanding, no doubt; but that unlimited love is what we are called to imitate in the preferential option for the poor. In the letter to Philemon, Paul writes on behalf of Onesimus, a slave. The apostle calls the slave his "son" and makes a touching plea to Philemon, "I am sending him, that is my own heart, back to you . . . with trust in your compliance. I write to you, knowing that you will do even more than I ask" (1:12–21). This is a stirring appeal on behalf of a runaway slave, with expectations of a gratuitous and unlimited response—"even more than I ask."

It is this kind of gratuitous love, also expressed in the Gospel and in first letter of John, that is at the theological core of the preferential option. Our term *preferential* has to do with this unlimited love. That is the fundamental basis for our preference for and commitment to the poor. Again, it is not that the poor are good and loving; rather, it is that God is good and loving.

Option

I would like to move now to our third term, *option*. The word for *option* in Spanish is usually considered stronger than that in English. There is some debate around the precise meaning, but it is clear that *option* means "a free decision," with implications for decisive action. The option for the poor is a free decision. Even more for a Christian, it is a conversion.

Conversion, in the Bible, implies two things: first, to leave one route, and second, to take another. That, in short, is conversion. That is what the option for the poor is: to leave one way of being Christian and to take another way. While such an option is a free decision, at the same time, it is a requirement for every one of us—even very good people. It is incorrect to understand the option only as an option for the poor by the nonpoor. The option is for everyone—nonpoor and poor. Many poor have not made the option for the poor. But to be committed to the poor and the alleviation of poverty is a requirement for poor people, also. Certainly, the option of the poor for the poor will be different from the option of the nonpoor for the poor. But the difference is not due to a different calling. We all have the same calling, the same duty—the option is a demand for every Christian—nonpoor and poor.

How do we make this option? How do we fulfill our Christian duty toward the poor? To opt for the poor means, in some way, to enter into their world. That is necessary but not easy. Let me offer a few observations and even some cautions. The "world of the poor" is a rhetorical expression, but let me try to clarify. The poor belong to a culture, a race, a nation, a gender, a class, and within these structures, they carve out a manner of being human. But within and, perhaps, because of these structures, little things, cultural characteristics emerge. I have found some of these to be important, from a pastoral perspective.

One point involves a different notion of time. When I arrived in my first parish, many years ago, I had, as any priest would, my watch and my calendar book. When parishioners would ask to see me, I would respond, "Of course," and take out my calendar and say, "Is Friday 11 a.m. good for you?" And, inevitably, it was always good. The poor are rich in time—they do not have work! They always said yes to whatever time I would propose. Little by little, I learned to be more flexible with time. I could no longer think that because I was important, my time was important—"Be here at 11:00, not 11:15 or 12:15." It simply did not work. The poor have a different notion of time.

Let me illustrate further some of the cultural implications of this notion of time that I have observed in my pastoral work. In my country, Peru, there are very few good roads in the Andes. It is difficult for the poor Indians to get transportation to another town. It has always impressed me to see poor Indians at car and truck stops waiting a whole day or maybe even two or three days. They sleep there and wait for a car or truck and simply jump in whenever one arrives. It is so different for us. If we are going somewhere by train or plane, we want to know exactly the hour and minute that the train or plane will arrive and exactly the hour and minute that it is scheduled to depart. If is a little late, we are frustrated.

Likewise, I have noted this different concept of time by observing the presence of the poor in the numerous downtown churches of my home city, Lima. During the day and evening, poor people are in the churches for thirty minutes, an hour, even two hours. They might not always be praying—some are; some are simply resting or escaping the hot sun. The churches are one of the few places where the poor can sit and rest. Nonetheless, the poor go there and spend a lot of time kneeling or sitting with Rose of Lima, Martin de Porres, Mary, and the suffering Christ. I have observed this often. Only after long periods do they go back out into the street. I am not claiming that this represents formal prayer time, as we might define prayer. My only point is that the poor spend long hours reflecting on their lives and their problems, praying a little, maybe sleeping, but what is apparent is a very different notion of time.

You might not think this relevant, but for me in my pastoral work, it is extremely important. This is the kind of understanding that we need to take into account in our preferential option for the poor. And that understanding, that deeper sharing of life, takes a long time. The caution I offer you is that sharing the life of the poor for a few weeks is good and can be helpful but please realize that it is not really entering into the world of the poor. It is only a glimpse.

To know a people, you need years of shared life with them. We must be clear about this point. There are no shortcuts, and some cultural and psychological characteristics run deep. The poor, as they struggle to survive in their milieu, feel and are "insignificant." That sense of insignificance is damaging—socially, psychologically, and spiritually. I had to realize that although I came from a very poor family, I was not insignificant. The reason is that I am a priest and, in my spare moments, a theologian. I am not insignificant; my cousins are insignificant. As I try to understand and opt for the poor, I must remember that.

Being poor means being defenseless and insignificant, and this recognition presents us with conflict. No one chooses to be insignificant. Coming from our different backgrounds and families, we cannot opt for insignificance. Moreover, we should not. We need to realize that to enter the world of the poor is not to become one more poor person. You can't, I can't, and we should not want to. Clarity is important here. To be committed to the poor is not to try to mechanically imitate the life of the poor. That is impossible. Certainly, we need to commit. We need to take on some form of poverty, some personal poverty, some austerity. But we must realize that for most of us, it is impossible to really share the life of the poor. However, that is not bad. The quest is not for us to be poor. Poverty is a scandal; it is never good. We should enter that world to get to know it, not to imitate it. We should enter that world to become committed—to fight against it.

Archbishop Romero was committed—he sought to protest the killing poverty that he saw around him. But he knew that he was not able to be really poor. I remember once being invited to lunch with him. He lived modestly and shared some of the austerity of the poor, but it was a nice lunch, not extravagant but much better than the poor would have. Nonetheless, he moved closer and closer to the poor—his people. Likewise, Ignacio Ellacuria, SJ, and his Jesuit brothers in El Salvador stayed close to the poor and were deeply committed to them. They constantly moved closer and closer to the poor, but they, too, knew they could not fully enter the world of the poor. They were not insignificant. As a matter of fact, I have never met an insignificant Jesuit! But they had made the option. And that should be our goal.

PREFERENTIAL OPTION AND
THE ANNOUNCEMENT OF THE GOSPEL

The preferential option that we have been discussing can be understood and implemented on a number of levels. There is, first of all, the practical social level. This level concerns our reaching out and walking with the poor. It is about the distribution of our time, energy, personnel, and material resources on behalf of the poor. It concerns our commitment in justice. This level is key and perhaps primary, but it is not all that the preferential option is about. More important, there is also the theological dimension of our option for the poor.

It is this level that I want to discuss here. Indeed, it brings together all of what we have discussed. My first point is that poverty is not only a social question; it is also a theological question. This theological level emerges because poverty is a direct challenge to the Christian message. It is a challenge that goes back two thousand years and needs to be faced by each historical period, each generation. Theology does not begin with social questions. It begins with questions about God, creation, sin, redemption, Jesus Christ, church, and sacraments. All of these themes are challenged by poverty, by the suffering of the innocent.

Some years ago, a young Colombian man who was studying theology in Rome came to interview me. He wanted to write a dissertation on the theology of liberation. He sat down with his pad and pencil and asked, "What are the main themes of liberation theology?" I looked at him and said, "There are many: God, creation, sin, redemption, Jesus Christ, resurrection, Spirit, church, sacraments . . . " He stopped taking notes. Apparently, he was waiting for a new revelation, but I told him, "That, I don't have!"

I relate that anecdote to indicate that different theologies only have to do with the manner in which the great themes of Christian revelation are presented and reflected on. The preferential option for the poor is the manner and lens through which the Gospel is announced by a theology of liberation. The option comes not only from the energy and force of Christians working with the poor. The option is also a way of finding Jesus. It is the way to be a disciple. It is a spirituality that helps us understand Jesus Christ and the God of Jesus Christ. It is our effort to grasp something of the gratuitous love of God for all of us and, especially, the poor.

The Dutch pastoral theologian Henri Nouwen, who taught here in the United States, wrestled with this option and its theological dimensions. During the early 1980s, he spent time in Peru, reflecting on the poverty there and the challenge it presented to our Christian faith. For him, the struggle was profound and personal. It was both internal and external. It challenged his understanding of Jesus and his church. It challenged his theology. Unfortunately, Nouwen died suddenly. But his diary, *Gracias: A Latin American Journal* (1983), beautifully describes his vocational struggle to witness to the Gospel among the suffering poor.

My second point concerning theology and the option for the poor is a simple and direct one. Theology, for it to be good theology, must be helpful. It must help the church announce the Gospel, announce Jesus in useful contemporary language. If theology is not helpful in that task, it is not theology. We theologians need to keep this in mind.

Moreover, we need to be clear about our reasons for wanting to announce the Gospel. There are many, of course. St. Matthew's Gospel ends with the great commission: "Go, therefore, and make disciples of all nations" (28:19). But there are other reasons. For me, the main reason for wanting to announce the Gospel is to share my joy—to share the reason for my joy. When we are joyful, we want to share that joy; we want to be with people; we want others to be part of our joy. For Christians, the main reason for our joy is the gratuitous love of God shown to us in the Gospels. If we are not joyful, we are not with God. To announce, to communicate, that Gospel is not just to announce ideas or words; it is to announce the ultimate source of our joy—a loving God.

In like manner, the preferential option for the poor is the lens that liberation theology uses to focus the announcement of the Gospel in our new century. The option is a way to announce Jesus's message and reveal the ultimate reason for our profound joy—the gratuitous love of God for all of us and, especially, the suffering poor. And that option has other, maybe unexpected, outcomes. By opting for the poor, we likely will find our joy increased. The poor, in spite of their suffering, are joyful. My parishioners know how to have a fiesta. If we reach out to the poor, we too might find joy.

Let me close by returning to my opening question. "How can we tell a poor person that 'God loves you'?" I am convinced that this can be done only by announcing the Gospel of God's gratuitous love through the preferential option. In this way, we share God's word and our deepest joy. The prophet Joel illustrates this realization of joy amid the most devastating circumstances. Poverty and suffering were catastrophic. Judah was ravished by an invasion of locusts. Starvation, death, and despair were everywhere. But Joel depicts the people praying for deliverance. And in the face of certain destruction, God does not fail in his love. He does not abandon his people. Israel is restored, and joy emerges from the ruins: "The mountains shall drip new wine, and the hills shall flow with milk" (4:18).

For us to grasp true freedom, liberation, and joy—even in the face of adversity and suffering—we need ultimately to understand something of the gratuitous love of God. This is the reason for our joy and the reason for our announcement of the Gospel. It is also the reason for our option to stand in solidarity and protest with the suffering poor of the world.

DISCUSSION QUESTIONS

1. Discuss the difference between "poverty as scandal" and "poverty as spirituality." How would you define and describe poverty? What does Father Gutierrez mean when he says that poor people are "insignificant"? Do you know any poor people well? Does his reflection help you to view the poor differently? How?
2. In your own words, using examples, discuss the three key terms: *preferential*, *option*, and *poor*.
3. What does Gutierrez mean by the "gratuitous love of God"? How might his approach to theology "help the church announce the gospel"?

RESOURCES AND FURTHER STUDY

Brown, Robert McAfee. *Gustavo Gutiérrez: An Introduction to Liberation Theology.* Maryknoll, N.Y.: Orbis Books, 1990.

Cadorette, Curt. *From the Heart of the People: The Theology of Gustavo Gutiérrez.* Oak Park, Ill.: Meyer-Stone, 1988.

Ellis, Marc H., and Otto Maduro, eds. *The Future of Liberation Theology: Essays in Honor of Gustavo Gutiérrez.* Maryknoll, N.Y.: Orbis Books, 1989.

Gutiérrez, Gustavo. *The God of Life.* Maryknoll, N.Y.: Orbis Books, 1991.

———. *Las Casas: In Search of the Poor of Jesus Christ.* Maryknoll, N.Y.: Orbis Books, 1993.

———. *On Job: God-Talk and the Suffering of the Innocent.* Maryknoll, N.Y.: Orbis Books, 1987.

———. *The Power of the Poor in History.* Maryknoll, N.Y.: Orbis Books, 1983.

———. *A Theology of Liberation: History, Politics, and Salvation.* Rev. ed. Maryknoll, N.Y.: Orbis Books, 1988.

———. *The Truth Shall Make You Free: Confrontations.* Maryknoll, N.Y.: Orbis Books, 1990.

———. *We Drink from Our Own Wells: The Spiritual Journey of a People.* Maryknoll, N.Y.: Orbis Books, 1984.

Nouwen, Henri J. M. *Gracias! A Latin American Journal.* San Francisco: Harper & Row, 1983.

Scorza, Manuel. *Garabombo, the Invisible.* Translated by Ana-Marie Aldaz. New York: Lang, 1994. Originally published in 1972.

5

Dead Man Walking:
The Journey Continues

Helen Prejean

JOURNEY TO TRUTH

In the opera based on *Dead Man Walking*, an amazing journey is musically and emotionally unpacked. The aria sung by my character is "My Journey, my journey to the truth . . . " And it truly is a journey to truth, climaxing in a high note of profound feeling. What the audience members don't know as the opera opens is that the real journey is going to be taken by them. The reason is that we haven't found a way to bring people close to the death penalty, to allow them to somehow identify with what happens in that high-pitched moment of execution. So, we turn to the arts, to film, and to books. Opera goes further, and by bringing together drama and music, it touches parts of our hearts that we don't even know we have.

When Teilhard de Chardin was writing *The Divine Milieu*, he came to the phenomenon of music and didn't know whether to put it in a spiritual category or a material category. He realized that the sound waves hitting our ear drums can change the spiritual state of our souls. It is mysterious how the juxtaposition of certain notes that are put together in a certain way can affect our souls so deeply. That is what happens in the opera; the audience is brought on a journey and gradually jolted to truth. As the opera begins, the audience members are traumatized as they watch two beautiful young people being murdered. They are killed right there; that is the prologue.

Everything uncoils out of the killing of those two young people. The traumatized audience is then hit by the next scene, a fierce juxtaposition, because it shows my character in the St. Thomas Housing Projects, in New Orleans, with children clapping and singing, "God will gather us around, all around. God will gather us around. Father and mother, sister and brother, God will gather us around." It is like an unbelievable fairy tale. It sounds like a little sing-along that you teach children, but given what the audience has just seen, the killing of two human beings, who can possibly believe that any force has the power to "gather us around"?

At this point, that part of us that demands justice in the journey comes forth. That demand for justice is enforced when the audience meets the killer. They don't like him. He is not remorseful and not repentant, and, of course, then you see the nun. You know that she's naïve; you know that she doesn't know what she's doing; you know that she is going to be conned. To be honest, that really helps, because I did not know what I was doing. Moreover, when you have a naïve person who is entering into something new, step-by-step, it really provides a graceful way for the audience to be able to come along with her.

But there is another part of our hearts that struggles with the death penalty because we hear about the death of innocent people. We feel outrage, and we should feel outrage. It is part of moral decency to be outraged when we hear about the death of people. Everyone who is sitting in the audience at the opera is going through this. Everyone has seen the killing, and there is a part of each of them that wants that final justice that we call the death penalty.

The opera keeps ratcheting, ratcheting up to the execution. And, finally, it comes. The murderer's family has said good-bye. It's time. They bring the man to the gurney; they strap him on. It's positioned upward, so you see that it's like an inverted cross. You cannot hide the shape of the execution gurney. And he is executed in a minute and a half of silence—the longest amount of silence ever in an opera. The audience is forced to hear the machines as they take over a human life and then kill it. And, still, he lies there. How are you going to end such an opera? There's a profound stillness that comes over the audience as everyone watches the death, hearing the sound of one's own heart beating in one's own ears. It is the sound of one's own soul watching a live human person being killed.

The way that the opera ends is perhaps the only way that it could end. The Sister Helen character comes in. There's the gurney. It's almost like a pietà. She faces the audience and sings, "God will gather us around, all around. God will gather us around." God is the life force and the gathering force that makes us community. We are one family, brothers and sisters; we cannot cut anyone out of the web of life. But, there is no denying that other part of us, the one still saying, "Yes, we can cut that one out; we can cut that one out." And that's the way the opera ends.

It is really a journey to truth—a story of awakening. I would like to turn now to some other stories of awakening.

STORIES OF AWAKENING

To be awake and to be set on fire with passion is the greatest grace that we could ever have. Awakening comes in different ways. Sam Ryan, a Jesuit from India, gave us a retreat and talked about his own awakening. He took a whole year off and just studied the Bible and the revelations about life and justice that he discovered there. He helped me immensely with his insight that the first revelation of God's heart in the Bible is in the burning-bush story about Moses. Even though Genesis comes chronologically first, Exodus was the heart of the experience of Israel. At the burning bush, God's heart is revealed to Moses; he finds God and commits himself to God's suffering people (2:23; 3). It is here that Moses heard the cry of his people and responded. It is the same cry that we need to hear. The bush is still on fire—burning hot. But can we see it? Can we feel the heat? Do we hear the cry? Can we respond?

The first story is about a young man, an African American studying theology in the Northeast. I remember when I read about his life. He had grown up in Atlanta in the Southern Baptist tradition and how amazed he was when he discovered the Bible and how the stories moved beyond a literal sense and opened a whole new perspective for him. He realized that these were stories of grace and power. They were metaphors that he could apply to his own life and the society around him. Then, he met a young woman, and they were married, and he was faced with a choice. He was given a professorship, and he could have stayed in the Northeast. It was the time of the Jim Crow days and terrible segregation in the South. The chance to settle in the North and in the academic world must have been attractive. However, he and his wife made the choice to pastor in a little church in Montgomery, Alabama.

One day, one of the women of the church, one who was looked up to for her wisdom and her faith—Rosa Parks—refused to go to the back of the bus. I have friends that have the small oak table from that church in Montgomery. I have often reflected on how small it is—only a few people fit around it. That reminds me of the working definition of *justice*, "just us." Work for justice always starts with a little bitty group of people. That small oak table is where that young pastor sat with a deacon or two and some of the leaders of the church to decide "What are we going to do about Rosa Parks?" They got the word out around the community with a simple note (there was no e-mail in those days): "Don't ride the bus." They had no idea if they could carry out the no-ride plan for even one day, much less for one week. But that little bitty group ignited the civil rights movement in the United States. Of course, you recognize that the story is that of Dr. Martin Luther King Jr.

My next story is also about a pastor, a priest who became a bishop. He started out as a serious seminarian with deep love for the church. The theology that he learned was the theology that some of us are old enough to have learned. God should be first in your life, and our task is to help bring the Kingdom of God. One day, we will all go to heaven. If you suffer during this life, you endure it with God's grace given by Jesus on the cross. It was a theology, above all, of charity: be charitable to one another; never question justice too much. But charity was important; prayer was important; having a life rooted in God was important; and most important of all, the holy Roman Catholic Church was the voice of God in obedience. The young priest prayed, studied, and helped the poor. He was given positions of responsibility, and he eventually got to be a bishop. As a bishop, of course, he became involved with the donors of the church, the wealthy people of means who were supporting the church, building the churches. There were dinners and banquets—the usual fund-raisers for charity. His homilies at Sunday mass were considered spiritual, sincere, and pure. People sensed that his love for people was genuine.

The bishop had a close friend, a younger priest, who was involved with the poor and their struggles. Poor people were getting killed when farmers tried to organize for their rights because wealthy landowners controlled most of the land in the country. Farmers tried to organize and to speak up for their rights, but more and more, the poor were being killed or were simply disappearing. The army was siding with the wealthy and oppressing the people. The young priest would talk to his friend the bishop and say, "Look, I was over with this group of people. This is what is happening to them" and "Do you know María and José? Their children have disappeared. Their sons are gone now. José, the father of the family, he's been killed."

Then, one day, the young friend of the bishop was brutally murdered, along with an old man and a young boy. That bishop, of course, was Oscar Romero. We often remember him from the moment he woke up. We remember him for what followed after he heard the cry from the killing of his friend Rutilio Grande, the priest who was his friend, the one who told him the stories, the one who went out and risked his life. That death literally cracked him open.

I was just in Australia. The aboriginal people have been there for thousands of years. They learned fire-farming. Millennia ago, they learned that burning some patches of land can render good results. There are some seeds that crack open only in fire, and only then will green sprouts grow. A few months later, the farmers can come back. Kangaroos would be grazing there and they could hunt. Only fire cracks open some seeds; so it was with Oscar Romero. He grew and he woke up. Rutilio Grande's death opened the seed of Oscar Romero's life. It was not long after he woke up that he stood before the people and told the members of the army, "Do not kill your brothers and sisters." Shortly thereafter, he was killed.

One more story: There was a nun once who came from an affluent family whose father was a lawyer. She grew up as a young girl in the South and had African American people as her servants. By the time that she was fifteen, she had gone to Europe. She had certain gifts. She went to a wonderful school, a private school taught by sisters. By the time that she was a junior in high school, she excelled at public speaking. She was the student body president. She made a lot of A's on her report card. As a child bride of Christ, aged eighteen, she entered a convent. She proudly wore the habit. Once, she even caught her habit on fire from an Advent wreath, which gives new meaning to "cracked open by fire." She knew from the faces of the fourth graders who yelled, in chorus, "Sister, you're on fire!" And in more than one way, she was on fire, wanting to be a saint. As a novice, she practiced silence and prayer, was the first one at chapel in the morning, sometimes making the Stations of the Cross before mass. She urgently wanted to love and practice charity, wanted to be a saint. During Lent, she kept a book tracking her work on different virtues: "This week I'm working on hope." "This week I'm working on humility." Each effort would get a checkmark.

She wanted the interiority, but she was very much an extrovert; so, she had to work at it. She finished the novitiate, made her vows, and was sent off to teach in a grammar school, seventh and eighth grade. At that time, bulletin boards were put up in the school that proclaimed "Come Holy Spirit" because there was something going on in Rome called the Second Vatican Council. The young sister pushed the students to pray for the success of the council: "Come, Holy Spirit, enlighten your church." However, she didn't have a clue about what she was praying for except that the church needed to be renewed, whatever that meant.

Not long before the council convened, Pope Pius XII had called on the religious orders to send 10 percent of all of their religious down to Latin America to serve. And, so, her community sent five sisters who wanted to be missionaries. They had no training. They just sent them to go and witness God to the people of Latin America.

After several years, the impact of Vatican II came. Her community took the recommended changes seriously. They called religious women to go back to the Gospel and to look back in history about why their community had been founded. Religious women, more than anyone else, took Vatican II to heart. Sisters went back to school and began to study. Community life changed. Nuns everywhere read the documents of Vatican II that said, "The joys and the hopes, the grief and the anxieties" of the world should be the joys, hopes, and grief of the church. The suffering of the world is our suffering. No more were we to escape from the world and to be in our convents; we were to join the people, to be with the people. It was liberation for the young nun. She was waiting for that liberation to happen, and when it did, she was able to open herself. You know, no more blind obedience to superiors: "Whatever you say, Mother; that's the will of God for me." But, instead, she could use her mind, use her gifts to begin to discern. Ignatian spirituality played a big role. Sisters and laypeople began to make directed retreats. The young sister did the thirty-day spiritual exercises of St. Ignatius. But still she struggled with change.

THE SEED BREAKS OPEN

During the 1970s, our community was just getting into the debate that the council provoked. Some of our sisters were coming back from Latin America and telling their stories. They explained that as missionaries, as long as they taught the children catechism, prepared them for the sacraments, and that was all, no one noticed; there was no persecution; nothing happened to anybody. But one of the nuns, Sister Margie, worked with a young priest, Father Hector, who was beginning to understand liberation theology. He was not only reading the Gospel to the people but working with the *campesinos* and showing the relevance of Jesus's message. "Why is it that eleven families should own 90 percent of all the land? Why are your children dying before they're five years old? You work for a pittance, and your children are starving. You have a right to demand what you need to live in dignity." The priests and sisters were organizing poor farmers into co-ops, and instead of just letting their crops be taken by the landowners, they were bringing them to market so that the people could get some profit from their own hard labor. Then, one night, Hector disappeared; he simply disappeared. They were all together when a truck drove up, and Hector was taken out of the tent. They never saw him again.

Again, it was the seed being broken open by fire. The priests and sisters realized that when they connected the Gospel to the needs of their people, the persecution, the oppression, the killings started. When the sisters applied the words of Mary's Magnificat to the rich and poor around them, they began, in fact, to suffer with the people they were serving.

As these stories made their way into our community throughout the 1970s and 1980s, things came to a head. We decided to gather as a group and wrestle with the question "What is being asked of us? And why is it that so many of us now are with the affluent and the middle class and are not directly involved with the poor?" Showing a preferential option for the poor became a rallying cry, but the debates went on. And this young sister was in the middle of the debate—she took the side of what was called the *spiritual* camp. The other side was called the *social justice* camp. The debate was hot and heavy. She strongly represented the spiritual side in the discussions, proclaiming, "We're nuns, not social workers. If the poor have God, they have everything. Didn't Jesus say, 'The poor you will always have with you.' Has it not always been the case that there have been rich people in the world and poor people in the world, and if the poor embrace their suffering with Christ, then one day they will be rewarded in Heaven?" As I am sure you have guessed, that young nun was Sister Helen—me. That is why, to this day, I am always humble when I am with my community because everyone knows where I have come from. They remember me—"I'm spiritual; I'm not political. I'm above being political."

It was at that time that I was introduced to the writings of people such as Albert Nolan, Oscar Romero, and Marie Augusta Neal. At a community meeting in Indiana, I listened to Neal and was moved. I got it. She told us that "integral to the good news that Jesus preached was that the poor would be poor no longer." To follow Jesus meant to follow the path of justice. The Catholic option for the poor means that you do not accept poverty; you resist poverty.

I began to read the Gospels more carefully. I read the lives of the saints differently. If Jesus had been a dreamy spiritual preacher that just gathered people together, announced the love of God, told them to whip out their guitars, sing "Love one another right now," and go home, they never would have crucified him. But, instead, he inaugurated a new project in history, a new kind of community where everyone was to be treated with dignity. Children, who were not even considered persons, just little bodies to be sent out to the fields to work, were given a special place. Women were his disciples; he worked with women and talked to them in public. He ate supper with the clean and unclean. He touched lepers. Everybody was treated with dignity. And no one was left in need. In the end, that is why Jesus was executed: his approach to life was an affront to authority—religious, political, and economic. His project had everything to do with justice. The young nun sat there, and finally, she got it.

I must admit that I was stricken because the journey had taken me so long. To be a person of charity was one thing, but to be a person of justice meant resisting injustice and working to change things. That was what the following of Jesus meant, and so I had to do it. I took simple steps; they were not complicated. As they say in Latin America, "the path is made by walking." That became my mantra. I moved into the St. Thomas

Housing Project. That is the way that *Dead Man Walking* begins. There, I got behind the curtain of the great American dream, and for the first time, I sat at the feet of people who had been my servants, and now I was their servant working in an adult learning center.

I learned a great deal at Hope House—the adult learning center—about school dropouts, welfare, and health care. I saw a man die on the street right there in St. Thomas because when the ambulance was summoned, the paramedics realized that he did not have medical insurance, so they turned around and left him to die. I saw the little trees planted to commemorate the drive-by shootings of children. Every time there was a gunshot, the mothers would run out, screaming, "Where is my child?" I remember Geraldine, one of the mothers, telling us, "My boys, something's happening to my boys. They're walking different, they're talking different." And I remember all the mothers who have lost sons. I can still see young girls coming into the adult learning center, fifteen years old, rocking their little babies like a doll saying, "Now, I have something of my very own." That is how I finally got Jesus's message. That was the fire that cracked open the seed.

DEATH AND VICTIMS: A SECOND BAPTISM

The seed was opened and the soil was tilled. I was able to stand on the shoulders of many people. They were already there. They had awakened ahead of me; they formed a bridge. Sister Lori Shaft had a program where she invited other religious to come spend time during the summer to live among the people and listen to their stories. She called it "Pathways through Poverty" and led participants through the criminal justice system, the welfare system, and the health care system.

We set up a similar program, called "Bridges." Five hundred young people from around the United States came to St. Thomas for one week. They did not come to build houses; they did not come to do anything. They came to sit at the feet of poor people and listen. They heard from people such as Rufus Smith, about how his son was shot by the police. Sister Lori had gone with him to the police station because the one thing that he wanted was the clothes of his dead son. He wanted to get the T-shirt that would show that his son had been shot in the back. They almost got away with it. They were that close when the police announced, "Sorry, we can't give you his clothes." Rufus Smith walked away from the police station brokenhearted because he could not prove that the police had shot his son in the back.

Everybody had somebody in prison. When I was growing up, we talked about what colleges people were attending. At St. Thomas, it was like "what prison?" I realized there was a greased rail from this poverty and being African American in this society to our state prison. It was in that atmosphere that one day, I got an invitation to write to a man on death row.

I began learning about the death penalty. I began to take my first steps. I took part in some protests and demonstrations. In early 1982, I wrote a letter to Patrick Sonnier. Two and a half years later, he was executed by the State of Louisiana. I witnessed it. He had said to me, "Sister, you can't be there because it might scar you." I responded, "Patrick, look at me, look at my face. I will be there for you. I will be the face of love for you. I will be the face of Christ for you because Christ doesn't want us to do this." He did look at me before the state killed him, before it put the mask over his face to protect the witnesses from seeing what happens to a human face when nineteen hundred volts of electricity are passed through one's body.

I did not know that when I stood there as that mute witness at the foot of that cross, it would be a second baptism for me and that I would be changed forever. I knew that my call was to be faithful and to show him a face of love—and I did that. I made it clear I was not a witness for the state. I was not complicit in any way with this brutal act of the state. I was there for him; I came out of the death house at about one o'clock in the morning; it was very dark It reminded me of Mark's gospel when he writes about the passion and death of Jesus, "Darkness came over the whole land" (15:33), and I threw up. I had never seen a human being killed in front of my eyes, and I thought, "What am I going to do?" Everybody thought that the death penalty was a great idea. Eighty percent of the people of Louisiana favored it then. However, I began to realize that they were never going to see what I just witnessed. The death penalty is a secret ritual. I had been brought in as a witness, and my mission and my job now were to witness. So, I began to tell the story.

I spoke to any group that would hear me. One important encounter really stands out—a sociology class at Loyola University—a captive audience. It was in that class that I learned about what I now call *both arms of the cross*. In my lecture, I talked about what had happened to Patrick Sonnier, his human rights, what Amnesty International said, what the UN Declaration of Human Rights said, why the death penalty was torture. I concentrated on what he had said before he died, his whole journey of transformation, and how he had come to God through this. I spoke with passion about the injustices that were part of the death penalty. When we came to the question period, the kids were on their feet in anger, saying, "You're not talking about the victim's family. You only talk about the human rights of this guy that did this crime. What about the victims? What about the victims? What about the victims?" I began to realize, right there in that classroom that I was not talking about the victim's family, that I was not talking to the victim's family. It hit me like a ton of bricks. Again, like the fire breaking open the seed, it felt like the greatest mistake of my life. I thank God for those Loyola students.

I had visited with Pat and his brother Eddie but had not once reached out to the families of those murdered, the families who had lost two teenagers. Even worse, I had only met them at the pardon board, which is the worst possible time to meet families because the situation is so polarized. When you go into a pardon board hearing, which is public in Louisiana, you sign the book indicating which side you are on. It always seemed to me like being in a Roman amphitheater. You give your thumbs-up—that is, you sign that you want the person to live or you are seeking clemency on the defendant's side (very few people)—or you give the thumbs-down that you are on the side of the state and you want to see the execution proceed (most of those present). That was when I met the victim's family. This is what I described in *Dead Man Walking*, the story of coming to the victims.

My editor, Jason Epstein, said to me, "If you don't talk about the crime in the first ten pages of this book, people are not going to read your book. They are going to say that you're a spiritual advisor to this guy, you're a nun, you're in sympathy with a murderer, and you're not going to be honest about what he did." And so, I learned from the victim's families. The first family that I tried to talk to was rightly very angry about the loss of their daughter; they wanted nothing to do with me, and they have never wanted anything to do with me. But, oh boy, the second family surprised me with their heroic grace. Both husband and wife moved me profoundly. They lost their son, but still, that Dad came up to me and said, "Sister, our son was murdered. All this time, you've been with these brothers, Pat and Eddie Sonnier, and you didn't want to come to see us. You can't believe the pressure we're under with the death penalty."

Revelation—I was in front of the flame again and being cracked open. I thought all victims' families were for the death penalty. I stayed away from them because of cowardice, because I was scared, because I did not know how to handle it. My wonderful Jewish editor became a spiritual director for a moment. I showed him the first draft of *Dead Man Walking*, where I had downplayed reaching out to the victims' families because I had never done that before. He looked at the text and said, "Well, Helen, it was cowardice, wasn't it? You were scared, weren't you?" I responded meekly, "Yeah." And he said, "Look, when you write your book, don't just take people on the peaks and waves when you do everything right. Take them with you into the troughs and ditches when you do something wrong."

Well, it was clear to me that I needed to correct that big mistake. That is what I try to do as I travel across the country. I realize how important it is to feel and absorb the outrage over a crime, to feel outrage when an innocent person has been violated and ripped out of life. I am learning to stand in the tension of the cross, both sides. I want to challenge and support people who say that they want to follow the way of Jesus and be on both arms of the cross. The victims' families need the dignity, accompaniment, and healing that does not leave them alone, before we can expect any understanding of the perpetrator. Likewise, we need to find ways to expose the perpetrator to the anguish and suffering of victims' families. You cannot short-circuit the journey that is involved in the death penalty in the United States. Most people experience deep ambivalence. We read about a mother and her children carjacked and killed or an elderly couple murdered, and we will feel the rage, and we should feel rage. In honesty, the outrage is real, and we cannot short-circuit it. We have to own it and respond to it.

Jason warned me that if on any page of the book, I let the tension collapse between the two arms of the cross—victims and perpetrators—the message would be lost. When William Faulkner was awarded the Nobel Prize for literature, he said that the only thing worth writing about is the conflict of the human heart. Jason drove his point home: "If you let the tension collapse between the horror of what Pat and his brother Eddie did to those kids and that family and the horror that the state and our government are now doing by torturing and executing a live human being, you will lose it all."

The torture was there, but our Supreme Court has yet to acknowledge it. When it's the law, we forget that it can be torture. Supreme Court decisions in the Furman and Gregg cases that brought back the death penalty said that it is not against the dignity of a human person to be executed even when we have as an alternative life imprisonment. It is not against one's dignity, not torture, they say. We came really close to continuing to kill kids, a five–four vote, but look at the four dissents. They are chilling because they are saying that states, if they want to, can execute kids; the Constitution, on its face, does not prohibit them from doing so. If you follow the thinking of Scalia, Rehnquist, O'Connor, and Thomas to its logical conclusion, by their interpretation, Alabama, for example, could literally hang ten-year-olds. That is their thinking.

Likewise, the justices seem unable to recognize the notion of mental torture. It is not enough that we keep people in death-row cells smaller than the cells at Abu Ghraib; we add to the extreme mental anguish. Take the story of Dobie, the first story in my new book *The Death of Innocents.* He was brought into the death house three times, the first time getting within an hour of death, but he got a stay of execution. He was brought back to his cell for a month, brought back to die. He said his good-byes to his family, and again, an hour and a half before his death, he got another stay of execution. He went back to his cell for a week, again brought back to die. Even the CIA and Abu Ghraib rules drew a clearer line: you can tie people up in excruciating positions for forty-eight hours; you can make them stand for seventy-two hours; you can deprive them of sleep for seventy-two hours; and you can deprive them of medication and food—but you cannot threaten people with immediate death. Nonetheless, our Supreme Court cannot recognize this mental torture. Yet, the United States signed the UN Convention against Torture, which defines not just physical torture but mental torture as well. Amnesty International gives us a good working definition of what torture is: the extreme mental or physical assault against those who have been rendered defenseless. We torture, but we do not recognize that we torture.

A BOOK AND A MOVIE: ANNUNCIATIONS

And so, the journey continued for me. It was exciting but not always pleasant. Pat Sonnier was executed. Robert Lee was executed. Willie Celestine was executed. That is when I decided to try to write a book. Many people were saying, "You ought to write a book," but why another book? There were many books on the death penalty, both pro and con. People read Rush Limbaugh when they are for it and Amnesty International when they are against it. However, now with hindsight, I can admit that I had no idea of the power of a book, but I knew that I had to do something bigger to get out the message. So for two years, I went into a cave and wrote a book. My provincial was a little bewildered, but she supported me. I was invited to meet an editor in New York, but I did not have funds for the trip. But my good Catholic mama came through, "Honey, look, I'm going to get you a suit. You get a nice suit, and you go meet that editor in New York." I stayed with a friend from Amnesty International. When I went to that meeting in New York, I didn't have a clue about publishing.

It was another step. Goethe said that when you are committed to a cause and unswerving in your commitment, providence begins to work for you, and resources make their way to you. That is what happened when I walked into Random House. Again, the naïve nun blunders into the big leagues. I met Jason Epstein, a creative and understanding editor. We had one of the best discussions on the death penalty that I have ever had in my life. I expected him to end by saying, "Thanks very much for coming to see us, Sister. We'll let you know." Instead, he simply said, "We'll do your book." I was flabbergasted. Jason Epstein showed me how to shape *Dead Man Walking* in a way that would bring people into the story. He personally got behind the book, presented it to the Random

House salespeople, and said, "This is going to be a book that will help change the mind of America about the death penalty, just like Rachel Carson's *Silent Spring* changed our view of the environment."

Later, I learned that a book is like a child. It has legs and takes on a life of its own. This one chose to fall into the lap of Susan Sarandon. She called me on the phone. I knew who she was because Amnesty had said that she was a great worker for human rights. But I knew nothing of her films. Friends told me to rent *Thelma and Louise*—that was my introduction.

When we really did meet, she said to me, "We need a film to awaken America; we need a film to deepen the reflection." Again, I was the novice; I knew nothing about films. I couldn't even remember if she played Thelma or Louise. It took Susan nine months to convince Tim Robbins to read the book. But one night walking down a street in Manhattan with him, Susan burst into tears and said, "Tim, if we're not going to do that film, we have to turn it over to someone who will." Robbins gave in, "Okay, Susan, I'll read the nun's book." She wore him down. After that, I read the wedding feast of Cana in a new light. Time for a miracle; they don't have any more wine. Push. Now. Now's the time. Mary pushed Jesus; she wore him down. People push us all the time. It's good and can be miraculous when it gets good things done.

Tim wrote the screenplay, but every Hollywood studio turned it down. They told him, "Tim, it's a downer. The guy did a terrible crime. He's guilty. He's going to be executed at the end. We've got no romantic element. We've got a nun in it with the death row inmate. If you let us spice it up, maybe we could get a film out of it, but it could never be a box office success. People don't want to reflect this deeply in America. They want entertainment. They want romance." But Robbins insisted, "It's about redemption." Yet, Hollywood still didn't get it. Finally, one company did. Polygram Film International agreed to produce *Dead Man Walking*. While Tim was editing, I remember asking him, "How are we going to get a lot of people to come see our movie?" He responded point-blank, "We're banking on some Academy Award nominations."

"But, Tim," I said, "that is such a long shot."

"Helen," he replied, "the whole movie is a long shot."

The big night—the miracle—did come, and there were 1.3 billion people watching. Bruce Springsteen sang the title song "Dead Man Walking." The film, along with Sean Penn, Tim Robbins, and Susan Sarandon had all been nominated for Oscars. Susan won an Oscar, and the film won many people over. It was the feast of the Annunciation. For me, it was the power of the Gospel. The Gospel was announced in a different way, and when you are a part of something so big, even though you may just be a little drop, a wave, a power rushes through you, and all that you can do is pray and be humble. I know that my gift is a little one, being given as part of something much bigger. But, as with Archbishop Romero, that is what we are all called to do. As the poet Mary Oliver asks us all, "what are you doing with your one wild, precious life?"

THE COURTS AND CAPITAL PUNISHMENT: WHAT CAN WE DO?

The journey continues for me. I do what I can. I am now with the seventh person on death row, Manuel Ortiz. He is a completely atypical person for death row in Louisiana. He comes from a wealthy military family in El Salvador. He is also totally innocent. However, for the prime years of his life, ages thirty-five to forty-six, he has been sitting on death row. He was accused, convicted, and sentenced to death for supposedly hiring somebody to kill his ex-wife for insurance money. After many years, the hearings are just being held that are beginning to show his innocence. As you might imagine, because his family was military and wealthy, his view of what was going on in Central America differed greatly from mine.

After about two years of visiting, we reached a point of crisis. I was about to explode. We had such different views about who Jesus is and about the killing and disappearance of poor people in his country that I could not continue. I told him, "I'll visit you, but I just don't want to be called your spiritual advisor." As a kind of parting gift, I sent him a book on Oscar Romero. The impact that Romero's story had on Manuel was earth-shattering. It cracked him open. He said, "If I do get off of death row, I'm going to spend my life on the side of the poor." That was the conversion of Manuel Ortiz. I see him now; I accompany him.

I met a woman on death row in Texas, Cathy Henderson. She should not be on death row in Texas. Two Christmases ago, I got a letter from her and then visited her and other women awaiting their fate. She said, "I have to prepare myself for the worst if they execute me. Will you be with me? I think you could help me be calm." Her story is a sad one of panic. She was baby-sitting, and the baby was crying. To calm the baby, she began swinging it around. She was barefooted. It was summer. There was a toy in the middle of the floor that had a sharp nail. She stepped on it and lost her balance. The baby flew out of her arms, hit the wall, and was killed. It all happened in an instant. The baby was dead, and she panicked. She fled. She acted out the fears of her own family background. Her mother had nine children with nine different men. Whenever her mother was in trouble, her mother fled. Cathy told me, "I did something stupid. I panicked; I fled." She buried the baby and ran to another state. Now she is on death row. The prosecutor in Harris County, her county, has half of all the women on death row and the highest percentage of people on death row. He has made her a monster and has vigorously gone for the death penalty. Today, she sits and waits on death row.

Being a spiritual advisor to somebody on death row means connecting the spiritual to other needs. I have been working with people to assemble "innocence teams" for people such as Cathy Henderson to help her get that autopsy and get a neuropathologist to look at exactly what happened on that tragic day. People are coming forward; the innocence teams are coming together. This is a new phase in the journey. This came about because I realized that I have now accompanied two innocent people to their execution, Dobie Gillis Williams and Joseph O'Dell.

The innocent being executed—how do you tell that story? That is the task of my new book, *The Death of Innocents.* Joseph O'Dell's story is amazing. In a Virginia prison, he waited eleven years for the state to allow an evidentiary hearing and a new DNA test that could prove his innocence. The appeals were refused. The story is really about the courts. When he defended himself at trial, a jailhouse snitch (surprise!) was brought in and testified, "He did it." His story has all the makings of the horror stories that we hear of the 118 wrongfully convicted people who have come off death row. Because the lawyers in the direct appeal to the state supreme court typed one wrong word on the document, Virginia refused to look at any of the issues of injustice that happened at his trial. It is hard to believe that that happens, but it does.

Procedure, procedure, procedure—that is what dominates the system all the way to the Supreme Court. What counts is not always the substance of what happened but rather the procedural flaws. The criteria have tightened up so much for constitutional protections that few defendants can access them. For poor people, it has become almost impossible to prove ineffectiveness of counsel, even when lawyers were drunk, when lawyers were on drugs, or when lawyers did nothing at a trial. The criteria made proof impossible. The words of Jesus were right on: "You strain out gnats and swallow camels while neglecting the weightier matters of justice and mercy."

This is the legal stage on which Justice Antonin Scalia performs. As disclosure, I should point out that Justice Scalia goes duck hunting with my brother Louie in Louisiana. Nonetheless, his views on the death penalty reinforce the vindictiveness and scapegoating of that part of our criminal justice system. He presented his views at a conference in Chicago in 2002. There, the justice held forth on his approach to the Constitution and his theology. When I read the transcript of the conference, I was astounded. He goes to Mass every Sunday, but he is selective in his use of the Bible to uphold the death penalty. He appeals to Romans: "But if you do evil, be afraid, for it [authority, rulers] does not bear the sword without purpose;

it is the servant of God to inflict wrath on the evildoer" (13:4). Scalia seems to think that it is God's will that state governments execute people.

Every Bible-thumping preacher in the South who wants to uphold the death penalty has been quoting that passage from Romans from the beginning. But a Supreme Court justice of the United States? That is astounding. Of course, the justice then has to engage in some fast footwork, saying that individual Christians have to forgive and should not hate. But he clearly thinks that divine authority to kill has been handed over to governments. He even expresses some nostalgia for monarchy: "In the good old days, when you had kings fighting wars with the Lord of Hosts behind them to determine the outcome, then we knew we had divine authority in government, but now with democracy, with these rogues and fools, we are doing our own will. We are not doing God's will." So, it seems, in Scalia's view, the more Christian a country is, the freer it is to execute. The reason that Europe does not execute is that it is post-Christian. "It has followed Freud, and it has not followed Christ." These are his words.

It is important to note that whenever Justice Scalia holds forth, he is always in charge of the venue. If anybody dared question him, as you could see at this conference in Chicago, the questioner was palpably nervous. Scalia would throw technicalities, disarm, make jokes; he was in charge. There was no discernment. Laughter ripples through the audience as he describes his God of wrath. Only one person in that conference stood up to him. An African American man, as I later found out, stood up toward the end and said, "I just want to say, Justice Scalia, I'm really worried that somebody like you sits on the Supreme Court. I have been beaten, and I have been in prison, and I know people on death row right now who have been beaten by the police, and they were coerced into signing false confessions. I'm worried that somebody like you . . . " And, of course, Justice Scalia tried to disarm him by saying, "And your question, sir?" The man responded, "I don't have a question. I just have a comment. I'm worried that somebody like you is on the Court." And then the moderators took over and deflected the questions. The man's name was David Bates. He was the only one who gave his name, and he said, "I'm worried." He was courageous; but remember that this scene took place in Illinois, where Governor Ryan was also courageous and took a stance of conscience and commuted all the sentences on death row. David Bates knew those prisoners.

We must continue the discourse. It is all about open, honest discourse. Thurgood Marshall, Supreme Court justice and African American, said that the American people say that they support the death penalty; but that opinion is not a reflective one. Educate the American people about the death penalty, and they will reject it. That is what we are working for:

many people across the country have been doing this work steadily, consistently, and we are beginning to see change. For example, in New Jersey, amazing new possibilities are emerging—namely, the New Jerseyans for Alternatives to the Death Penalty.

Let me conclude with one last initiative. Tim Robbins has written a stage play of *Dead Man Walking*. This is not for Broadway; it is for high school and college students and for parish groups. This year (2005), it has been piloted in Jesuit schools in Chicago, Dallas, and New Orleans. The play is produced and directed by students. The death penalty is suffused throughout the curriculum. Some schools are doing art programs; some are doing music programs. The play has unleashed unbelievable creativity, getting the discourse going around all aspects of the death penalty. In Houston, where the play is going to be performed, Bishop Fiorenza, who has stood strong against the death penalty all these years, will hold a seminar on the death penalty for his priests, deacons, and seminarians; after, they will all see the stage production.

The play will be especially helpful for college and high school courses that want to discuss faith and justice issues and for parishes that want to deal with the controversy surrounding the death penalty. When we discuss the death penalty, we need to be clear that the Catholic church has changed its teaching on the death penalty. The church's stance is substantive; it is a principled opposition to the death penalty. There are no exceptions. People need to know that. But they need also to know some of the stories of death row inmates and some of the stories of faith-filled people who have changed their views on the death penalty. Most of all, they need to be exposed to both arms of the death penalty cross—death row prisoners and victims' families. We need to talk about it and how the teaching has changed and how people in congregations can make the journey. Tim's contribution has been a godsend; the stage production and curricular impact have been a great way to get young people and parents involved. The play's script is a great way to further the discourse—to continue the journey.

DISCUSSION QUESTIONS

1. As a group, discuss Sister Helen's journey to truth. Have any of you ever been "cracked open by fire"? What was it like? Give examples. Did it change you? How?
2. Have you or your community experienced violent crime? How did you handle it? How did the victim's family handle it? Did being a follower of Jesus, a victim of the death penalty, affect the way that you deal with crime and punishment? How?

3. Opposition to the death penalty seems to be gaining some support; what might you as an individual or as a parish group do to help the effort? Can your group arrange to show and discuss *Dead Man Walking* or support the play project described by Sister Helen?

RESOURCES AND FURTHER STUDY

Catechism of the Catholic Church. Rev. ed. Libreria Editrice Vaticana (Vatican Publishing House); Mahwah, N.J.: Paulist Press, 1997. See, in particular, nos. 2265, 2266, 2267.

Catholics against Capital Punishment. Website (for newsletter and updates). www.cacp.org (accessed May 2, 2007).

Dead Man Walking. Film. Directed by Tim Robbins. Polygram Film International, 1995.

Fenlon, Maureen. *Dead Man Walking School Theatre Project.* Blog. dpdiscourse.typepad.com/playproject/.

Hopcke, Robert H. *Catholics and the Death Penalty: Six Things You Can Do to End Capital Punishment.* Cincinnati, Ohio: St. Anthony Messenger Press, 2005.

John Paul II. "Statements of the Holy Father on the Death Penalty." Comments made in St. Louis, January 1999. Social Development and World Peace. http://usccb.org/sdwp/national/criminal/stlouissmt.htm (accessed May 2, 2007).

Overberg, Kenneth R. "Respect Life: The Bible and the Death Penalty Today." *Scripture from Scratch* (October 2000). www.americancatholic.org/Newsletters/SFS/an1000.asp (accessed May 2, 2007).

Prejean, Helen. *Dead Man Walking: An Eyewitness Account of the Death Penalty in the United States.* New York: Random House, 1993.

———. *The Death of Innocents: An Eyewitness Account of Wrongful Executions.* New York: Random House, 2005.

———. *Welcome to Hell: Letters and Writings from Death Row.* Chicago: Northwestern University Press, 2004.

United States Conference of Catholic Bishops. *Catholic Campaign to End the Death Penalty.* www.usccb.org/sdwp/usccbdpstatements.shtml (accessed May 2, 2007).

———. *A Culture of Life and the Penalty of Death.* Washington, D.C.: United States Conference of Catholic Bishops, 2005. http://usccb.org/sdwp/national/penalty ofdeath.pdf (accessed May 2, 2007).

6

The Color of Money:
Racism and the Economy

Diana L. Hayes

DREAM AND REALITY

Forty years ago, the Reverend Martin Luther King Jr. observed,

> When the Constitution was written, a strange formula to determine taxes and representation declared that the Negro was 60 percent of a person. Today another curious formula seems to declare he is 50 percent of a person. Of the good things in life he has approximately one half those of whites; of the bad he has twice those of whites. . . . There are twice as many unemployed. The rate of infant mortality . . . is double that of whites (quoted in Muhammad et al., *State of the Dream*, 22).

These words, written in 1967, can still be read as truth in the United States today. If anything, the situation for many, especially for African Americans and immigrant Latinos and Latinas, has actually worsened. How is it that in the first decade of the twenty-first century, we find ourselves in the wealthiest country in the world as a nation that finds itself incapable of providing for the least among us, the poor, the elderly, those with physical and mental challenges; the list of inadequacies is almost endless.

THE OLD NEW DEAL

Just over sixty years ago, a promise was made to the American people by President Roosevelt, a promise that should haunt us to this day, for it has not been kept and it continues to be ignored by those presently in office. In his State of the Union of January 11, 1944, FDR presents an economic bill of rights to the American people:

> It is our duty to lay the plans and determine the strategy for the winning of a lasting peace and the establishment of an American standard of living higher than ever before known. We cannot be content, no matter how high that general standard of living may be, if some fraction of our people, whether it is one-third or one-fifth or one-tenth, is ill-fed, ill-clothed, ill-housed, and insecure. . . .
>
> We have come to a clear realization of the fact that true individual freedom cannot exist without economic security and independence. Necessitous men [and women] are not free men [and women]. . . . In our day, these economic truths have become accepted as self-evident. We have accepted, so to speak, a second Bill of Rights under which a new basis of security and prosperity can be established for all—regardless of station, race or creed. (quoted in Rosenman, *The Public Papers*, 40–42)

Roosevelt lists a number of these rights, including the right to a remunerative job, a just or living wage, a decent home, adequate medical care, a good education, and adequate protection from the economic fears of old age, sickness, accident, and unemployment. This second bill of rights would seem to be something that all Americans would support for one another. But if that is so, why are we in the situation that we are today where forty-five million Americans are without health insurance, where many of our senior citizens find it necessary to continue working at minimum-wage jobs to make ends meet, where sixteen million persons with health insurance hesitate to use it because of the high deductibles and co-pays that are involved, where the infant mortality rate for blacks is still twice as high as that for whites, and where unemployment, even in these times of prosperity, has increased to two and a half times that of whites? The statistics go on and on showing the still-yawning gap between rich and poor, black and white (see American Friends Service Committee, *What Is Economic Justice?*). How can this be so today?

We need to look behind the words to the reality of the New Deal and what actually took place and how it was implemented, rather than dwell on just the words that were spoken. Language can be deceptive; words are easy to use. Putting action behind those words is something else again. Sadly, in the United States, we must recognize time and time again that the language of equality continually falls victim to the praxis of racism, which has been a sickness eating away at the core of our being since the founding of this nation.

As the late Supreme Court justice Thurgood Marshall noted at the U.S. bicentennial in 1976, "what is the meaning of the three words 'We the People' that serve as the preface to our Constitution?" They certainly did not include women, who were denied the vote, but neither did they include blacks, male or female, each of whom only counted as three-fifths of a person. This biased accounting boosted the voting power in Congress of those very states that bought, sold, and profited from the denial of humanity to an entire people, those of African descent. Latinos and Latinas as well as Native Americans were, of course, not even thought of at this time. No, the root of the economic inequality that still exists in these United States can be found in the particularly heinous form of slavery that was imposed on persons of African descent in the earliest decades of our existence as both a colonial and a national entity.

We are still dealing with the inequalities that emerged from maintaining one group of people as livestock based simply on distorted interpretations of the Old and New Testaments. This led to the denial of humanity of so many human beings and the denial that we all are all made in the image and likeness of God.

From slavery through a pseudo freedom to Jim Crow with its tainted laws that continued to justify humanity's inhumanity to other men and women, we see the reason why blacks and other persons of color still find themselves lagging behind persons of European ancestry in this country. Although anyone with 1/32 of African blood was considered black and innately inferior for over four centuries in the United States, we should remember that the concept of whiteness only came into existence to counter the existence of black people. To be white was to be, by definition, a free person, a superior being. Ironically, however, many who today bask in their whiteness and its accompanying privilege may not be aware that their ancestors had to earn that designation; it was not automatically given. The Irish, Jews, Italians, Greeks, and countless other ethnic and racial groups had to be declared by U.S. courts a part of the so-called white race to earn the benefits and privileges of whiteness. As a result, many were deceived into turning against those who were just as poor as them for the assumed benefits of white skin (see Ignatieff, *How the Irish Became White*). King noted so eloquently in "I Have a Dream,"

Not logic but a hollow social distraction has separated the races. The economically depressed white (who I might add still exists and is even multiplying in numbers especially in our rural areas) accepts his poverty by telling himself that, if in no other respect, at least socially he is above the Negro.

Yet, if we are truly honest with ourselves, we all know that . . . God never intended one people to live in superfluous and inordinate wealth, while others know only deadening poverty. God wants all of his children to have the basic necessities of life, and he has left in this universe "enough and to spare" for that purpose.

Yet, the gap between the rich and poor continues to grow exponentially, with 1 percent of the wealthiest in this nation having its share of wealth double while the poorest 20 percent having their share decrease.

What happened to FDR's promise? What went wrong? The New Deal proposed by him in 1935 was admirable in its commitment to relieve the economic hardships of a nation in a seemingly unending depression. Unfortunately, the promises made were compromised. Race and its accompaniment, racism, could not be ignored, especially "away down south in the land of cotton." An egalitarian commitment was confronted and all too easily defeated by an uncompromising racism, the fruit of slavery, which was determined to keep the "Negroes" in their place, under the feet of white men and women.

For all intents and purposes, African Americans were deliberately left out of the New Deal programs. It was done subtly but also, when necessary, blatantly. To ensure that the Democratic South would support his innovative programs of social uplift and security, President Roosevelt had to acquiesce to the demands of the Jim Crow South, which was insistent on the preservation of its right to maintain its "peculiar institution" of latter-day slavery, or feudal sharecropping.

Katznelson notes that "the South's representatives . . . used three mechanisms" to ensure this course of events:

> First, . . . they sought (whenever possible) to leave out as many African Americans as they could . . . by writing provisions that . . . were racially laden. . . . Categories of work in which blacks were heavily overrepresented, notably farm workers and maids . . . were excluded from the legislation that created modern unions, from laws that set minimum wages and regulated the hours of work, and from Social Security until the 1950's.
>
> Second, they successfully insisted that the administration of these and other laws, including assistance to the poor and support for veterans, be placed in the hands of local officials who were deeply hostile to black applications.
>
> Third, they prevented Congress from attaching any sort of antidiscrimination provisions to a wide array of social welfare programs such as community health services, school lunches, and hospital construction grants. . . .
>
> As a consequence, at the very moment when a wide array of public policies was providing most white Americans with valuable tools to advance their social welfare—insure their old age, get good jobs, acquire economic security, build assets, and gain middle-class status—most black Americans were left behind or left out (*When Affirmative Action Was White*, 23–24).

Katznelson correctly concludes, "Affirmative action was white. New national policies enacted in the pre–civil rights, last-gasp era of Jim Crow constituted a massive transfer of quite specific privileges to white Americans. New programs produced economic and social opportunity for favored constituencies and thus widened the gap between white and black Americans in the aftermath of the Second World War." The negative aftereffects of these actions remain to the present day, coupled with a seemingly renewed intent on the part of federal, state, and local governments to erase the slight gains that have taken place for blacks since the civil rights movement.

But let me put a human face on what I have just written. My mother, Helen Louise Dodson Hayes, granddaughter of an Irish Confederate colonel and a Creek Indian woman, both former slaves, had to leave school, to her everlasting shame and sorrow, in the sixth grade to go to work as a domestic to help her family of nine survive. From that time until I received my doctorate in theology, some fifty-six years later, my mother worked, for the most part, full-time, as a domestic, a baby-sitter, a maternity ward aide, a home health care attendant, and at other jobs, most of which did not provide a pension, social security benefits, or health benefits. When she applied for social security at the age of sixty-five, she received less than $200 a month. By the time that she died, much too young, at seventy-nine, it had increased to approximately $400. She lived on this and a pension of $31 a month, yet when she applied in the 1980s for food stamps, she was told she made too much.

This perpetual impoverishment of persons of color, especially for the young and the old, is the legacy of slavery and its child, racism. It has caused the loss to our society of men and women like my mother and father, who, had they been able to stay in school and attain higher education, would not only have bettered their own lives but those of countless others. And yet, a recent law signed by President Bush cuts drastically the funding available for loans and grants for college education to persons of the middle and working classes—those without independent means, who are the majority of people in our nation.

How do you catch up to others when your feet and hands have been deliberately tied and when the doors to opportunity are repeatedly slammed in your face, not for decades but for centuries? How do you address the now more insidious racism that exists in our country today, which smiles in your face while reaching around to stab you in the back as it claims to be color-blind?

FAITH, RACE, AND ECONOMIC JUSTICE

The issue of economic justice is not new or recent. Indeed, it is at the heart of the Catholic church's social teachings. However, it, like the presence of millions of persons of color in the church from its earliest beginnings, is still one of our best-kept secrets. Why? Why do we spend so much time on issues of doctrine and tradition that will not help to feed a hungry child, provide a father or mother with a decent day's pay for a hard day's work, or put roofs over the heads of families who are forced to live in shelters and cars in this, the greatest nation on Earth? We call ourselves "a nation of believers," but we seem to measure our greatness by the number of nations we invade, the number of countries we bully, the number of men and women who are killed.

Many of those who join the military services do so because they cannot find decent-paying jobs anywhere else. Is it not ironic that, allegedly, the most democratic and egalitarian workforce in our nation is the military, especially, the army. What does this say about us as a nation, supposedly, a nation of people who believe in God. I for one would be very afraid because the God I read about in Scripture is a God of justice who hates injustice and demands that the widow and the orphan, the stranger in our midst, be welcomed and cared for, not bullied and intimidated or denied the basic rights owed to all human beings. They are of God, whether black, brown, yellow, red, white, mixed, gay, straight, rich, poor, whatever—they are still human and we owe them respect for their God-given humanity.

For Christians, what is economic justice? What is it that we owe our neighbor? What is the "option for the poor"?

> It means building a fair economy that works for everyone (regardless of race, class, gender, creed or sexual orientation). It means fair trade policies that protect workers rights to organize and to receive a living wage for their work at home and abroad. It includes budget and tax policies in which corporations and the wealthy pay their fair share, and which support good schools and child care, affordable health care and housing, retirement security, and a safety net for those in need. It is based on a vision of economic human rights (American Friends Service Committee, *What Is Economic Justice?* para. 2).

And it is comparable to those rights promised by FDR in 1944, the right to food, shelter, and other basic necessities. Yet, the United States, again, the wealthiest nation in the world, has proven incapable of providing these basic rights to its citizens who need them the most.

The poor in our midst are real human beings living lives of quiet and sometimes not-so-quiet desperation at the prospect of their future and their children's future. However, too many of us are consumed by "bling-bling," buying, taking, acquiring, in whatever ways that we can, more and more stuff that we, in actuality, cannot afford and do not need.

What about the dreams of the poor in our midst? Does no one care about their hopes, their dreams, their desires, or are they not allowed to have them simply because they are poor? Their dreams are simple: food on the table every day, a roof over their heads, a little extra for the kids' new clothes and shoes. They don't even think of things such as iPods and laptop computers, yet many schools now require students to have access to these to do their homework and projects. At the same time, our libraries are being closed for lack of funding, both public and school libraries; our schools are deteriorating while demands are made to satisfy more and more government programs to wage war. How can you dare to dream of a future in a classroom whose windows are boarded up or nailed shut, where access requires going through a metal detector, where one's backpack has to be clear plastic or open mesh so that its contents can be seen, where no one has time to work with the slow or the gifted, where everything is geared toward the federally mandated test, which means life and death to students, to teachers, to entire school systems but does not provide our children with the skills needed for good jobs in today's world.

The poor are in our midst, but quite often, we don't really see them. Their presence offends us, when it should shame us. They are overwhelmingly women, single heads of households; they are overwhelmingly women of color; they are increasingly desperate.

Were you watching television in September 2005 when Hurricanes Katrina and Rita hit New Orleans and the coasts of Mississippi and Louisiana? Did you read the newspapers and news journals? I did and I saw how on every cover, whether that of *Time* or *Newsweek*, the *Economist* or *Der Spiegel*, the face of poverty, the face of despair, the face of hopelessness in the United States was the face of a black woman, usually with babies clinging to her as she stood almost submerged in foul and stinking waters. This was happening while our president observed from the safety of Air Force One, while he played on his new birthday guitar as New Orleans drowned, while he praised incompetents. Meanwhile, people desperate for food and water were being shot at or arrested as looters but only, for the most part, if they were persons of color.

Unfortunately, we as a nation have learned the lessons of our forefathers very well. If the victims are black or Hispanic, the situation is not critical. I must admit that a year ago, if someone had said this, I would have severely questioned him or her, but I cannot ignore—we cannot ignore—what is still taking place in the Gulf states as thousands remain displaced, having lost not just everything they owned but their livelihoods and loved ones. Moreover, they are still being told to be patient while they are still reeling from being shipped like cattle across the nation without input or concern for family.

Shades of slavery come back to haunt us. And, of course, blacks were the hardest hit in many ways because they already had the least; they could not evacuate because they did not have cars, gas, credit cards. But they did have chronic illnesses, lots of children, and the aged in their midst. Once again, those with the least have suffered the most.

In many ways, the state of our country today reminds me of the words of the prophet Ezekiel in his proclamation of God's anger and judgment:

> The leaders are like lions roaring over the animals that they have killed. They kill the people, take all of the money and property they can get, and by their murders leave many widows. The priests break my laws and have no respect for what is holy. . . . The officials are like wolves tearing apart the animals they have killed. They commit murder in order to get rich. The prophets have hidden these sins like men covering a wall with white wash. . . . The wealthy cheat and rob. They ill-treat the poor and take advantage of foreigners (22:23ff).

Does this not sound awfully familiar? Just read the papers and watch the nightly news.

We ourselves are the poor. The poor are not demons. They look like us, talk like us, and have dreams like our own. How many of us who are living a middle-class or higher standard of living are, in reality, only a paycheck or catastrophic illness away from losing everything? But we, at least, have resources that the materially poor do not have. Who, then, are the materially poor? Gustavo Gutiérrez provides us with a description:

> What we mean by material poverty is a subhuman condition. . . . The Bible also considers it this way. Concretely, to be poor means to die of hunger, to be illiterate, to be exploited by others, not to know that you are being exploited, not to know that you are a person ("Remembering the Poor").

The faces of those who are "materially poor" in the United States are predominantly female; they are black and brown and, yes, even white; they are children and teens, our grandparents and elderly aunts and uncles. Most of them work, but despite two or more jobs, they still can't make ends meet. This is not surprising in a country where to stay afloat, the average family requires both parents to work. Most of the elderly poor do not have pensions, even while greedy executives extract enormous salaries and retirement packages. The materially poor are the senior citizens and family heads working at McDonald's and Burger King on a minimum wage insufficient to feed two let alone a family of four. They are our past and our future. How can we continue to see ourselves as a nation of hope and prosperity in the face of starving, poorly educated, homeless, and medically uncovered men, women, and children who have lived and worked for generations in this land?

What our country and its people are doing is a denial of God's law and teachings. Pope John XXXIII wrote words that, perhaps, we need to be reminded of today:

Beginning our discussion of the rights of [humanity], we see that every [person] has the right to life, to bodily integrity, and to the means which are suitable for the proper development of life ; these are primarily food, clothing, shelter, rest, medical care, and finally necessary social services. Therefore, a human being also has the right to security in cases of sickness, inability to work, widowhood, old age, unemployment, or in any other case in which he [or she] is deprived of the means of subsistence through no fault of his [or her] own (quoted in Neuhaus, *Preferential Option*, 47).

These words are at the core of Catholic social teachings as well as sacred Scripture. The rights that Pope John asserts belong to all human beings, regardless of race or ethnicity, creed or lack thereof, gender or sexual orientation, or class status. They are an affirmation of God's justice, bestowed equally and generously on all of us, because and only because we are all human. It is a justice that is demanded of all of us as well when another million or so have slipped into poverty because of our refusal to raise the minimum wage, when the number of children in poverty is in the double digits, when race and poverty continue to be so intimately and blatantly linked.

Over twenty years ago, U.S. bishops issued a landmark document, *Economic Justice for All*, calling for change in our policies toward the least among us. They set forth in this document six moral principles. They held great promise and are still needed today:

1. that every economic decision and institution must be judged in light of whether it protects or undermines the dignity of the human person;
2. that human dignity can be realized and protected only in community;
3. that all people have a right to participate in the economic life of society;
4. that all members of society have a special obligation to the poor and vulnerable—this is what we mean by the "fundamental or preferential option for the poor"
5. that human rights are the minimum conditions for life in community; and last,
6. that society as a whole, acting through public and private institutions, has the moral responsibility to enhance human dignity and protect human rights.

For more than five hundred years in the United States, human and civil rights have been based, not on the basic dignity of all human beings who are all created equally in the image and likeness of God, but on distorted images of an allegedly superior humanity that denies that creation. We can no longer, if ever we could, afford the luxury of racism anymore than we can afford the luxury of sexism, classism, or heterosexism or any other socially constructed ideology used to promote a few at the expense of the many. The real measure of a nation is not its gross national product; rather, it is the number of hungry, the number of poor, the number of homeless, the number of those ignored, abused, assaulted, and denied the minimum rights of life. Given this, we as a nation and a people are truly damned. Ten years after the economic pastoral letter, the American bishops noted the existence of three nations in our midst:

> One is prospering and producing in a new information age, coping well with new economic challenges; A second is squeezed by declining real incomes and global economic competition. They wonder whether they will keep their jobs and health insurance. . . . A third community is growing more discouraged and despairing. Called an American underclass, their children are growing up desperately poor in the richest nation on earth. Their question at the end of the month is whether they can afford the rent or groceries or heat. . . .
>
> As people of faith, we believe we are one family, not competing classes. We are sisters and brothers, not economic units or statistics. We must come together around the values of our faith to shape economic policies that protect human life, promote strong families, expand a stable middle class, create decent jobs, and reduce the level of poverty and need in our society. We need to strengthen our sense of community and our pursuit of the common good. A decade after the pastoral, it remains clear that the moral test of our society is how the poor, the weak and the vulnerable are faring. And by this standard we are falling far short (United States Conference of Catholic Bishops, *A Decade after Economic Justice*, "Introduction").

Today, twenty years after the pastoral, the situation has not improved but worsened, especially among blacks, Latinos and Latinas, and rural whites. Studies show that racism still plays a critical role—for example, persons with black-sounding names, even with superior credentials, are 50 percent less likely to be interviewed for jobs than those with white-sounding names; whites with criminal records are more likely to be offered jobs than are blacks without records; the poverty rate of blacks in 2002 was three times that of whites; and one-third of black children live in poverty, as do one-fourth of African Americans as a whole.

The most important question is, what can we do about this situation? I fear that, from a government standpoint, very little will be done other than observing the decline while allowing it to continue. Likewise, from an ecclesial, institutional perspective, I am not optimistic. We lack anyone, it seems, whether in the churches or in political life, with the courage to address these issues in any serious and meaningful way. What these leaders fear, I do not know, other than stepping out and going against the prevailing trends.

These leaders are unlike Archbishop Romero, who, when exposed to the extremes of poverty and wealth in his homeland, refused to maintain a complicit silence with the rich and powerful. He spoke out with scathing denunciations of those in positions of civil, political, and religious leadership. He called on them to repent of their wrongdoing, of their selfishness and greed, and to recognize the suffering humanity in their midst. Today, in the United States, there are scattered voices of outrage but no voices that strongly condemn the materialism and greed rampant in our country, not even within our churches. Since the death of Martin Luther King Jr., martyred for his faith, as was Archbishop Romero, there have been few willing to name what others seek to hide.

CONCLUDING REMARKS

How do we reclaim the dream of American progress, proposed by Reverend King so many years ago, and bridge the racial divide that has impeded that progress for too long a time? How do we open the eyes of our fellow Americans to the harm that they are doing to themselves and their families by their resistance to equal opportunity for all Americans? How do we silence those in our midst who blatantly reveal their racist ideologies with their efforts to criminalize the poor, especially, the immigrants? They're willing to fence-in Mexico but ignore those coming into the country illegally through Canada because the latter are more likely to be of European origin.

The authors of *The State of the Dream, 2004* propose this solution:

> The money to invest in America can be found without raising taxes on the middle class by shifting spending priorities. We must end the hemorrhaging of America's wealth to the super-rich and use it to re-invest in America. We must also limit US military expenditures and, for a fraction of the cost, put funding at the service of all the American people. Dr. King would surely decry the ability of the federal government to find $160 billion [and it's much more now] for military intervention and occupation of a foreign country and, at the same time, claim insufficient funds for greater equality at home (Muhammad et al., 22–23).

These issues form just the tip of the iceberg. What must be asked and answered by the American people is in many ways a question similar to that raised just before the Civil War:

> Are we willing to see our nation founder on the basis of disproven lies that serve today only to divide and destroy us rather than to help us grow stronger? Either we are a nation united by our shared history, painful though it may be, as Americans, or a nation willing self-destruction because of our

overweening pride, greed, and contempt for our fellow citizens simply because they are and will always be different. The choice is ours; one way leads to grace, the other to self-destruction.

As Dr. King said at National Cathedral in Washington, D.C., on March 31, 1965, "there is nothing new about poverty. What is new is that we have the techniques and resources to get rid of poverty. The real question is whether we have the will."

DISCUSSION QUESTIONS

1. Do you know people who are trying to raise a family on a minimum-wage job, without health insurance? What do you think that would be like?
2. Discuss Dr. Hayes's point that after the progress of the civil rights movement, racism has become more subtle and more insidious. Why have we made people of color, especially women, bear the burden of prejudice? Do you see racism and prejudice in yourself, your family, your community, your church? How does it show itself? What does the response to Hurricane Katrina tell us about race relations in the United States today?
3. Discuss the six principles from *Economic Justice for All*. Why do you think American Catholics did not pick up on the message? Was Martin Luther King Jr. right about fighting poverty? He said that we have the "techniques and resources" but questioned whether we have the will.

RESOURCES AND FURTHER STUDY

American Friends Service Committee. *What Is Economic Justice?* www.afsc.org/economic-justice/learnabout.htm (accessed May 2, 2007).

Gutiérrez, Gustavo. "Remembering the Poor: An Interview with Gustavo Gutiérrez." By Daniel Hartnett. *America* 188, no. 3 (February 18, 2003).

Hayes, Diana L. *And Still We Rise: An Introduction to Black Liberation Theology.* New York: Paulist Press, 1996.

———. *Hagar's Daughters: Womanist Ways of Being in the World.* New York: Paulist Press, 1995.

———. "Speaking the Future into Life: The Challenge of Black Women in the Catholic Church." In *The Church Women Want*, edited by Elizabeth A. Johnson. New York: Crossroads, 2002.

———. *Were You There? Stations of the Cross.* Art by Charles S. Ndege. Maryknoll, N.Y.: Orbis, 2004.

———. "We Too Are America: Black Women's Burden of Race and Class." In *The Sky Is Cryin': Race, Class, and National Disasters*, edited by Cheryl A. Kirk-Duggan, 69–79. New York: New York University Press, 2006.

Hayes, Diana L., and Cyprian Davis, eds. *Taking Down Our Harps: Black Catholics in the United States*. Maryknoll, N.Y.: Orbis, 1998.

Ignatieff, Noel. *How the Irish Became White*. London: Routledge, 1995.

Katznelson, Iva. *When Affirmative Action Was White: An Untold History of Racial Inequity in Twentieth-Century America*. New York: Norton, 2005.

King, Martin Luther, Jr. "I Have a Dream." Speech. August 28, 1963. www.stanford .edu/group/King//publications/speeches/address_at_march_on_washington .pdf (accessed May 2, 2007).

Muhammad, Dedrick, Attieno Davis, Meizhu Lui, and Betsy Leondar-Wright. *The State of the Dream, 2004: Enduring Disparities in Black and White*. Boston: United for a Fair Economy / Racial Divide Project, 2004.

Neuhaus, Richard John. *The Preferential Option for the Poor*. Grand Rapids, Mich.: Eerdmans, 1988.

Rosenman, Samuel. *The Public Papers and Addresses of Franklin Delano Roosevelt*. Vol. 13. New York: Harper, 1950.

United States Conference of Catholic Bishops. *A Decade after Economic Justice for All: Continuing Principles, Changing Context, New Challenges*. Washington, D.C.: United States Conference of Catholic Bishops, 1995. www.osjspm.org/majordoc_us_ bishops_statements_economic_justice_for_all.aspx (accessed May 2, 2007).

United States Conference of Catholic Bishops. *Economic Justice for All*. Washington, D.C.: National Conference of Catholic Bishops, 1986. www.osjspm.org/ economic_justice_for_all.aspx (accessed May 2, 2007).

7

✢

A Promised Land, A Devil's Highway: The Crossroads of the Undocumented Immigrant

Daniel G. Groody

The great legacy of Archbishop Oscar Romero's life was his identification with the crucified Christ. While his witness to the God of life reached its ultimate expression during his last liturgy, the sacrifice of his own life on the altar of God was the culmination of his solidarity with those who suffer on the altar of the world. Among the many poor people for whom he laid down his life are those who eventually emigrated from his country in search of more dignified lives. As we reflect on the contribution of Oscar Romero's life, I would like to do so in light of what Ignacio Ellacuría calls "the people crucified in history." In particular, I would like to look at the physical, spiritual, and theological terrain of the undocumented immigrant coming across the Mexican-American border today.

The context of Romero's death leaves much room for reflection, but in the very least, it prompts us to consider the integral relationship that his faith expressed at liturgy and that his commitment to the poor expressed in the struggle for justice. As a starting point, I would like to look at the relationship between the Eucharist and immigration. While, on the surface, there does not appear to be an obvious connection between what happens at Mass and what happens on the border, the correlation became clearer the first time I attended a Eucharistic celebration in El Paso, Texas, where Mexico meets the United States. We celebrated Mass outside on November 1, in the open air, in the dry, rugged, and sun-scorched terrain where the two countries meet. In this liturgy, we remembered all the saints and the souls who had gone before us. We also remembered the thousands of Mexican immigrants who died at the crossroads of the border in recent years. Like other liturgies, a large crowd gathered to pray and worship. Unlike at other liturgies, however, a sixteen-foot iron fence divided this community in half, with one side in Mexico and the other side in the United States.

To give expression to our common solidarity as a people of God beyond our political constructions, we joined altars on both sides of the wall. Even while border patrol agents and helicopters surrounded us and kept a strict vigilance—lest any Mexicans cross over—we sang, we worshiped, and we prayed. We prayed for our governments. We prayed for those who died. And we prayed to understand better our interconnectedness to each other. I remember in particular the sign of peace, when one normally shakes a hand or shares a hug with one's neighbor. Unable to touch my Mexican neighbor except through some small holes in the fence, I became acutely aware of the unity that we celebrated but also the divisions that we experience. Even while this Eucharist testified to our unity in Christ, the wall between us revealed the dividedness of our current reality, for no other reason than that we were born on different sides of the fence.

A FAITH PERSPECTIVE ON A COMPLEX REALITY

For the last few decades, I have been talking to immigrants, border patrol agents, *coyote smugglers* (those who transport people across), ranchers, vigilante groups, educators, congresspersons, medical personnel, social workers, human rights advocates, and others involved in this immigration drama. Ranchers have seen their property trashed by immigrants who parade through their land and leave behind water jugs, litter, and discarded clothing. Educators and hospital administrators have felt increasing financial pressure from the influx of newly arrived immigrants. Border patrol agents have told stories of being pinned down by gunfire from drug smugglers of cocaine and marijuana. Congressional leaders have felt pressure, especially since September 11, to establish policies that aim at safeguarding a stable economy and protecting the common good. Coyote smugglers have talked about guiding people across the treacherous terrain along the border and gaining a profit while doing so. But most of all, migrants have shared what it is like to break from home, cross the border, and enter the United States as undocumented immigrants. In the process, they have revealed not only much about the physical terrain of the immigrant journey but also the spiritual terrain of their faith lives.

In speaking with these different groups along the border, I have learned that each constituency believes that it has certain rights. Each group has a point to make, a truth to defend. These include the rights to private property, jobs, national security, civil law and order, and other such rights. The legitimacy of each claim makes it clear that immigration is a complex reality and that it is not easy to untangle a web of competing interests. Yet, it is here that theology can offer some important reflection about what it means to be human before God and what it means to live together in society.

From a theological perspective, while every truth claim merits consideration, not every claim has equal authority. Christian theology asserts that, as a starting point, those who suffer the most deserve the greatest hearing (Matthew 25:31–46), even though, ironically, the voice of the "least" is often the last one to be heard, if it is heard at all. Oscar Romero learned throughout his life that the poor themselves not only deserve to be heard but are key to gaining an accurate grasp of reality, without which wise choices cannot be made. In the context of immigration, this is where the stories of the immigrants themselves are particularly important. As some of the most vulnerable members of society, immigrants clarify that whatever "rights" are at stake in this debate, one of the most neglected is the right to a more dignified life. These rights become clearer when one listens to the stories as they emerge from various crisis points along the border, including detention centers, hospitals, shelters, train stations, deserts, mountains, and along rivers and highways and other areas. Their stories have made me look at the immigration issue differently. They have helped me see that the journey of an undocumented immigrant is not a camping trip through a scenic part of the American Southwest but a descent into the vast expanses of hell; their journey toward a "promised land" takes place on what Luis Alberto Urrea calls "a devil's highway."

THE EVOLUTION OF THE
MEXICAN-AMERICAN BORDER

The pathways of this highway have been carved out slowly over time. The Mexican-American border has undergone a complex evolution, especially over the last century. Up until the end of the Mexican-American War in 1848, when Mexico ceded what is now much of the Southwestern United States, people moved freely and cyclically throughout the current border states and Mexico. The border area remained relatively porous, and enforcement was relatively light through most of the nineteenth and twentieth centuries, except for a vigilante organization in 1880 that tried to keep the Chinese out. In 1924, the U.S. Border Patrol began tightening the border through more systematic enforcement efforts. In time, stricter border policies emerged, especially in the 1980s when President Reagan declared a "war on drugs." This "war" made the border an increasingly militarized zone as American drug enforcement entities battled against wealthy, organized drug cartels for superiority in firepower and surveillance.

An important development for the border was the devaluation of the Mexican peso in 1983, which triggered an explosion of foreign-owned factories along the Mexican side of the border. U.S. companies took advantage of the exchange rate by moving their assembly plants from the states to Mexico in pursuit of cheap labor. Hundreds of thousands of Mexican citizens, many of whom had lost their land because of Mexican agricultural policies, came north to work in *maquiladoras*. In the last few years, however, more than a quarter of these plants have closed down as companies have discovered even cheaper labor in Asia. Consequently, hundreds of thousands of jobs along the border have disappeared, digging the Mexican economy into a deeper hole and making unemployment and underemployment more the norm than the exception.

In the 1990s, the Clinton administration, fueled by much anti-immigrant sentiment that was brewing in California such as that reflected in proposition 187, further intensified border control with policies such as Operation Hold the Line, in El Paso, and Operation Gatekeeper, in San Diego, and later, other similar initiatives. By erecting walls and fences, by stationing border patrol agents every quarter mile along the border in the major urban areas, and by the increased use of military technology, including drone planes, infrared technology, motion sensors, and other such instruments, crossing outside of normal ports of entry became much more difficult, which, by design, has significantly raised the stakes of migrating illegally. To avoid detection, immigrants are pushed to the most remote areas of the border where surveillance is thin.

While policies such as Operation Gatekeeper in 1994 and similar initiatives along the border were meant to deter immigrants from crossing illegally, they have not changed the flows at all but merely redirected migrants into more life-threatening territory, such as waterless deserts and mountains. With temperatures exceeding 120 degrees in the shade, many have to walk fifty miles or longer in treacherous conditions. In such surroundings, one's body cooks like an egg, which causes heat stroke, brain damage, and even death. Because it is physically impossible to carry the food and water necessary for this type of trek, many do not make it. I realized how extreme this journey was when one day, a coyote offered me a "ride-along scholarship" so that I could see what the journey was like. Instead of paying the going rate of $1,800 to take me across the border, he said he was going to "teach" me what it was like, for free. His words were as follows:

> We'll walk for three or four days, and all you will have with you are a few tortillas, some sardines, and water. The food is so bad you won't want to eat, and you will get so tired you won't think you are going to make it. If you push on, you can do it, but if you fall behind, we will leave you behind. And

you should wear high heel, leather boots, because we come across rattlesnakes in the desert at night, but if you have the right boots on, the snake's teeth won't penetrate your skin and you'll be okay.

Because of such dangers, every day, immigrants dehydrate in deserts, drown in canals, freeze in mountains, and suffocate in tractor trailers. As a result, the death toll has increased 1,000 percent in some places. When asked what he thought about the dangers, an immigrant named Mario said,

> Sure, I think about the dangers. I think about them all the time. But I have no choice if I am going to move forward with my life. The fact is, amidst the poverty in Mexico, I am already dead. Crossing the desert gives me the hope of living, even if I die.

If they make it across the border, most immigrants will work at low-paying jobs that no one else wants except the most desperate. They will debone chickens in poultry plants, pick crops in fields, and build houses in construction. As one person noted, "it looks like entering the U.S. through the desert as undocumented immigrants do is some kind of employment screening test administered by the U.S. government for the hospitality, construction, and recreation industries." Willing to work at the most dangerous jobs, an immigrant a day will die in the workplace, even while for others, the workplace has become safer over the last decade. Immigrants die cutting North Carolina tobacco and Nebraska beef, chopping down trees in Colorado, welding a balcony in Florida, trimming grass at a Las Vegas golf course, and falling from scaffolding in Georgia.

With an economic gun at their backs, they leave their homes because hunger and poverty push them to cross the border. Mario told me in an immigration detention center,

> Sometimes my kids come to me and say, "Daddy, I'm hungry." And I don't have enough money to buy them food. And I can't tell them I don't have any money, but I don't. I can barely put beans, potatoes, and tortillas on the table with what I make. But I feel so bad that I sometimes will go into a store, even if it is two or three blocks away, or even three or four kilometers away, or even another country in order to get food for my family. I feel awful, but nothing is worse than seeing your hungry child look you in the eyes, knowing you don't have enough food to give them.

Immigrants are pushed by economic poverty, pulled by the hope of a better life in the United States, and blocked by an iron wall at the border. At this border, where the ideals of freedom in America are safeguarded, many immigrants clash with a form of slavery embedded in the contemporary American imagination.

CROSSING THE BORDERS OF OUR OWN MIND

While many Americans hailed the crumbling of the Berlin Wall in 1989 and mourned the death of sixty-eight people who died trying to cross it over a period of twenty-eight years, many of us have stood idle as we have constructed a new wall between Mexico and the United States. Since 1994, more than 4,000 undocumented immigrants have died trying to find their way into America. The tragic loss of life along the Mexican-American border is a challenge to the national consciences of Mexico, the United States, and, indeed, the global community. While it raises serious questions about structural injustice, it challenges all of us to reflect on how we regard those labeled as "different" by mainstream society.

Despite the obstacles that immigrants face in crossing the border, perhaps the more difficult borders to cross today are the borders of our own minds, especially, those that guard our deep-seated biases and prejudices and those we put up when we encounter someone who we consider to be totally "other" than we are. Mexican immigrants bear some of the worst stereotypes in today's society and are some of the first to be typecast in a negative light. Not infrequently in mainstream media, they are typecast as illegal, nontaxpaying "leeches" who suck dry the funds of local communities while selling drugs, committing crimes, and taking jobs away from Americans. Some even lump immigrants into the same category as terrorists, as an unwelcome threat, without ever realizing that the terrorists of September 11 came into the country with legal visas. Nonetheless, in the popular mind, immigrants are perceived as a menace to the common good and the preservation of U.S. culture. Absurdly, some—apparently unaware of the last battle against indigenous Americans at Wounded Knee—argue that immigrants are taking away "Native American" culture.

Whatever one's perceptions about these popular impressions, sadly, many of the immigrants themselves begin to believe the stereotypes spread about them. Often looked at as uneducated, lazy, and inferior, they begin to internalize many of these labels. Such stereotypes have their origin from the time of the Spanish conquest in the early sixteenth century. Unfortunately, many immigrants come to believe some of the ways that contemporary society typecasts them. Perhaps, one of the more challenging roads to conversion for them is not only believing in God but believing in themselves. Lydia comments,

> We are constantly reminded that we are less than everybody else, that we are poor, that we don't have an education, that we don't speak right, that we are lesser human beings in one way or another. Sometimes, we even begin to wonder whether God thinks that way about us too.

The more challenging road to conversion for many Americans often means unlearning the negative stereotypes and seeing more clearly the inner worth, dignity, and respective contributions that immigrants bring to this country.

A DAY WITHOUT A MEXICAN

Despite the tide of anti-immigrant sentiment, the economic undercurrent is such that immigrants are an essential and vital part of our current economic reality. We have effectively walled off the truth about the role that immigrants play in sustaining the infrastructure of America. As Pastor Robin Hoover of Humane Borders says, "our nation virtually posts two signs on its southern border: 'Help Wanted: Inquire Within' and 'Do Not Trespass.'" Without the help of immigrant labor, the U.S. economy would virtually collapse. We want and need cheap immigrant labor, but we do not want the immigrants.

A few years ago an interesting documentary came out called *A Day without a Mexican*. It attempted to show what the American economy would look like if there were no Mexicans working here anymore. There would be no maids in hotels. No people to wash dishes in restaurants. No landscapers to mow grass. No cheap hands to do construction. No people to pick vegetables in the fields. As a result, lettuce would cost more than eight dollars a head; industries would shut down; various sectors of the economy would be paralyzed. Even though the U.S. economy needs these immigrants and even though multinational corporations profit from their labor, immigrants today are not afforded the same opportunities or open doors that immigrants experienced in previous generations. In fact, the opposite is true. Instead of receiving hospitality and openness, many immigrants find scapegoating and rejections, hostility and fear.

Today, some immigrants are greeted by vigilante groups and civilian border patrols who hunt them down, treat them like animals, and even threaten to kill them. In parts of the Southwest, racist violence runs deep in groups such as the Civil Homeland Defense, Ranch Rescue, and American Border Patrol (not to be confused with the U.S. Border Patrol). "If I had my way," one rancher reportedly bellowed at a meeting with U.S. Border Patrol officials, "I'd shoot every single one of 'em." The fact is that most immigrants are not stealing jobs from Americans; they are doing work that most Americans do not want to do. Moreover, not only are immigrants not a drain on the U.S. economy, but they also contribute with direct and indirect taxes. Even though immigrants collectively pay more than $90 billion in taxes, many are afraid to use social services for fear that it will expose their undocumented status.

Nonetheless, like previous immigrants from Ireland, Italy, Germany, Eastern Europe, China, and Japan, these Mexican immigrants, as Jorge Bustamante notes, are often valued for their cheap labor but are not afforded the human rights due to them as contributing members of society. They become a "disposable commodity" when they are no longer useful. It is here in particular that the Scriptures and Catholic social teaching have something important to say.

THE RELATIONSHIP OF IMMIGRATION TO REVELATION

According to the Judeo-Christian Scriptures, immigration is not simply a sociological fact but also a theological event. In the process of immigrating, God revealed his covenant to his people. This covenant was a gift and a responsibility; it reflected God's goodness to them, but it also called them to respond to newcomers in the same way that Yahweh responded to them when they were in slavery: "So you too must befriend the alien, for you were once aliens yourselves in the land of Egypt" (Deuteronomy 10:19).

Building on this same foundation, Catholic social teaching has reiterated that the true moral worth of any society is how it treats its most vulnerable members. John Paul II consistently underscored the moral responsibility of richer nations to help poor nations, particularly with regard to more open immigration policies. While some in America claim that these undocumented immigrants have no right to be here, the church believes that a person's true homeland is that which provides the person with bread.

When Moisés reached Tijuana, he said that the reason why he wanted to come to the United States was that he could barely put food on the table with what he earned. He said that his ambition was simply to provide "bread" for his family. On this same day, a few miles away on the other side of the border near a very popular resort hotel on Coronado Island, a woman said that she had come to the area because she was looking for a "specialty bread," a delicacy that she could not find anywhere else. The contradictions of the moment were striking: two people can live in the same geographical place but live in two totally different worlds. These two lives are microcosms of a larger contrast between Mexico and the United States, between the First World and the Third World.

While the church recognizes the right of a nation to control its borders, it does not see this right as an absolute right, nor does it see sovereign rights as having priority over basic human rights. It acknowledges that the ideal is that people find work in their home countries; however, it also teaches that if their countries of birth do not afford the conditions necessary to lead a fully human life, then those persons have a right to emigrate. While border reform does not mean naively opening our borders to everyone, as if there were no need to take into account other political and socioeconomic factors, the church makes every effort to put human life at the forefront of the discussion. It critically asks why barriers have been steadily lowered when it comes to commerce but have steadily risen when it comes to labor. If Oscar Romero were alive today, he would likely challenge those unjust social structures that benefit the elite at the expense of the poor or that calculate financial costs but ignore the human costs of economic systems and political policies. He would indict a society that values goods and money more than it does human beings and human rights, which directly contradicts the biblical narrative. While some Americans and some Christians may see our privileged life in the United States as a divine right, a scriptural reading of reality offers an entirely different perspective.

The gospel vision challenges the prevailing consumerist mentality of American culture, which seeks meaning through a seemingly endless accumulation of goods, even while the rest of the world suffers for want of basic needs. Jesus, in his life and ministry, went beyond borders of all sorts, including those defined by the authorities of his own day, such as clean/unclean, saintly/sinful, and rich/poor. In doing so, he called into being a community of magnanimity and generosity that would reflect God's unlimited love for all people (Acts 2). He called people "blest," not when they have received the most, but when they have shared the most and needed the least. Christians, as such, distinguish themselves not by the quantity of their possessions but the quality of their heart, which expresses itself in service. Above all, this quality of the heart is measured by the extent to which one loves the least significant among us.

In many respects, immigrants sit at America's door like Lazarus sat at the gate of the rich man (Luke 16:19–31), hoping for scraps to fall from the American table of prosperity. While there are many texts through which to analyze today's reality along the border, the Judgment of the Nations (Matthew 25: 31–46) is a particularly challenging text through which to read the issue of immigration. In this passage, Jesus says, "I was hungry and you gave me food, I was thirsty and you gave me drink, a stranger and you welcomed me, naked and you clothed me, ill and you cared for me, in prison and you visited me." The corollaries to the immigrant experience are striking. Hungry in their homelands, thirsty in the treacherous deserts in which they cross, naked after being robbed at gunpoint by *bandito* gangs, sick in the hospitals from heat-related illnesses, imprisoned

in immigration detention centers, and, finally, if they make it across, es-
tranged in a new land, they bear many of the marks of the crucified Christ
in our world today.

Migrants undergo a way of the cross every day. They experience an economic crucifixion when they realize that they can no longer subsist in
their homeland. They experience a social crucifixion when they have to
leave their families and friends behind. They undergo a cultural crucifixion when they leave behind the familiar and come into a new and strange
land. They experience a legal crucifixion when they cross the border and
become "illegal aliens." For those who die in the deserts and mountains,
they experience an actual crucifixion, dying some of the most horrible
deaths imaginable. And they even experience a religious crucifixion of
sorts when they experience themselves as strangers, outsiders, and even
threats to church communities, if they are welcomed there. As an archbishop, Romero was one that welcomed the excluded and put them at the
center of his pastoral attention and ministry. His own spirituality and
identification with the crucified Christ compelled him to go the poor as
his response of love to the God of love.

Spirituality and theology are built into the struggles of immigration,
particularly, migrants, even if the situation does not look that way on the
surface. John Paul II notes,

> The immediate reasons for the complex reality of human migration differ
> widely; its ultimate source, however, is the longing for a transcendent horizon
> of justice, freedom and peace. In short, it testifies to an anxiety which, how-
> ever indirectly, refers to God, in whom alone humans can find the full satis-
> faction of all his expectations ("Message for World Migration Day," no. 1).

What appears to be simply a sociological, political, and economic phenomenon has a deep theological current under the surface. Theology,
above all, engages the hopes and struggles of the human heart, and from
there, it seeks to find God's revelation in the midst of everyday life, even
and especially in those "godless" areas where God seems disturbingly
absent. Theology takes flesh in the ordinariness of life, and because it is
rooted in everyday life, it is also rooted in the everyday sufferings of
people.

Theology, as it is disclosed in history, has always evolved in this way.
While Christians today regard the cross as the one symbol that summarizes God's redemptive love for the world, at the time of Jesus, it held no
initial theological significance. In biblical times, the cross was a form of
capital punishment, which, in the Old Testament, reflected more of God's
curse than his blessing (Deuteronomy 21:23). However, upon deeper reflection, a theological truth emerged about the cross, symbolizing God's

self-giving love to God's people. In a similar way, migration, like the cross, has deep theological dimensions. Immigrants hold much potential to be bearers of new life. In response to the challenge of immigration, the U.S. bishops, as expressed in their pastoral letter *Strangers No Longer: Together on the Journey of Hope,* have sought "to awaken our peoples to the mysterious presence of the crucified and risen Lord in the person of the migrant and to renew in them the values of the Kingdom of God that he proclaimed" (Catholic Bishops of Mexico and the United States, no. 3). Building on this similar spirit, Romero not only reached out to those on the edge of society but realized that the church is born on the margins, where those who are crucified live and suffer today.

Amid such difficult conditions, many immigrants offer a surprising but compelling witness of faith. When María came north from Guatemala, she wanted to work in the United States for only two years, then return home to her family. I met her on the Mexican side of the border, just before her third attempt to cross. In the previous ten days, she had tried twice to cross the border through a remote route in southern Arizona. On her first attempt, she was mugged at the border by a *bandito* gang. Though bruised and beaten, she continued her journey through the desert and ran out of food. Just before she reached the road, she was apprehended by the border patrol and put into an immigration detention center. A few days later, she tried again. This time, her coyote smuggler tried to rape her, but she managed to free herself and push her way through the desert once again. After four days of walking, she ran out of food, water, and even strength. After almost dying in the desert, the border patrol found her, helped her, and then sent her back to Mexico.

After chronicling her story to me for a long time and after telling me about her suffering in detail, I was curious about how she dealt with these trials before God, so I asked her, "If you had fifteen minutes to speak to God, what would you say to Him?" Thinking that she would have given Him a long litany of complaints, María surprised me when she said,

> First of all, I do not have fifteen minutes to speak to God. I am always conversing with Him, and I feel His presence with me always. Yet, if I saw God face to face, the first thing I would do is thank Him, because He has been so good to me and has blest me so abundantly.

It is extraordinary to ponder that thousands of years ago, Israel's strongest affirmations about God's faithfulness often came in the midst of its own exile in Babylon, not in the midst of prosperity. Given that many immigrants live as exiles in the United States, it is striking to witness such faith amid such adversity and to see such revelation in unsuspected places.

MIGRATION AS A JOURNEY OF HOPE

Archbishop Romero understood that salvation was intimately inter-twined with a commitment to the crucified peoples of today. He testified to the mercy of God in a merciless world. "In my life," he said, "I have only been a poem of the love of God, and I have become in Him what He has wanted me to be." Standing in solidarity with Christ on the altar and through Christ as crucified with the poor, Romero came to be known as an *entregado*, one who not only gives one's life for his people but also re-veals through faithful witness the life of the Savior, known in Spanish as *El Salvador*. He also understood that following this Savior led him to a mi-gration of hope, even and especially when his labors for justice took place amid a seemingly hopeless situation.

As immigrants such as those from Mexico and other parts of Latin America fight for more dignified lives, it is helpful to remember that the term *immigrant* is built into the church's very self-definition. It sees itself as comprising a "pilgrim people" moving from sin to grace, from cross to resurrection, and from this world to the next. In the Eucharist, the church protests against the walls and barriers that we set up between ourselves, and it affirms again and again that we are one body in Christ. It realizes that, this side of heaven, we all live in the same country; we all live on the same side of the fence. To the church, death is the ultimate border; the journey of faith is the ultimate migration; and God is the ultimate prom-ised land. Christ teaches that we will be able to cross over this final bor-der to the extent that we have been able to cross over the smaller borders in this life and see our interconnectedness to each other (Luke 16:19–31). In the very least, we need a new imagination to bring about a new immi-gration policy.

Life itself, if we live it well, is a process of endless migration. Movement toward the promised land inevitably calls us to cross borders of every sort, and it makes us vulnerable in the process. As undocumented immi-grants remind us, this journey is not a road for the fainthearted. Each day, God calls us out of our comfort zones as we move from the known to the unknown, from the secure to the insecure, from the land of our physical birth to the land of our spiritual birth. It is only when we choose not to migrate, when we stagnate, when we seek to save our lives rather than lose them in God, that we spiritually die. If "migration" is worked into the self-definition of all peoples, then we might find those who come to us as immigrants less threatening than we often do. And we might see not only a reflection of ourselves but that of God, who, even when we were lost, did not abandon us to die. Rather, in love, God "migrated" to us in the In-carnation so that, through Him, we might migrate with Him across all

borders into the fullness of God's loving embrace and find our true homeland in God's Kingdom.

DISCUSSION QUESTIONS

1. Given the complexity of the immigration question, why do you think
   that the church has taken the stance of defending the immigrant—
   even the undocumented immigrant? Since most Americans are the
   offspring of immigrants, why do you think the anti-immigration sentiment is so strong?
2. Discuss: Have you had personal or business dealings with undocumented immigrants? Do they work hard? If legislation were passed
   that prohibited helping undocumented immigrants, would you be
   willing to break the law and still help them? Why? Why not?
3. How is the Eucharist a sign that breaks down walls and barriers?
   Discuss Father Groody's point that the term *immigrant* is "built into
   the church's very self-definition."

RESOURCES AND FURTHER STUDY

Catholic Bishops of Mexico and the United States. *Strangers No Longer: Together on
   the Journey of Hope.* Washington D.C.: United States Conference of Catholic Bish-
   ops, 2003. www.usccb.org/mrs/stranger.shtml (accessed May 2, 2007).
Elizondo, Virgil. *Galilean Journey.* Maryknoll, N.Y.: Orbis Books, 1983.
Groody, Daniel G. *Border of Death, Valley of Life: An Immigrant Journey of Heart and
   Spirit.* Lanham, Md.: Rowman & Littlefield, 2002.
———, prod. *Dying to Live: A Migrant's Journey.* Video/DVD. Notre Dame, Ind.:
   University of Notre Dame, 2005.
———. *Globalization, Spirituality, and Justice: Navigating the Path to Peace.* Maryknoll,
   N.Y.: Orbis Books, 2007.
———, ed. *The Option for the Poor in Christian Theology.* Notre Dame, Ind.: Univer-
   sity of Notre Dame Press, 2007.
Groody, Daniel G., and Gioacchino Campese, eds. *A Promised Land, a Perilous Jour-
   ney: Theological Perspectives on Migration.* Notre Dame, Ind.: University of Notre
   Dame Press, 2007.
John Paul II. "Message for World Migration Day." United States Conference of
   Catholic Bishops, November 21, 1999. www.usccb.org/pope/wmde.htm (accessed May 2, 2007).
Skylstad, William. "Comprehensive Immigration Reform." United States Conference of Catholic Bishops, January 15, 2006. www.usccb.org/bishops/immigration
   reform.shtml (accessed May 2, 2007).

Index

About the Editors and Contributors

Pilar Hogan Closkey is the executive director of Saint Joseph's Carpenter Society, Camden, New Jersey. Educated at the University of Notre Dame and the University of North Carolina, she is a professional planner and civil engineer and has published articles in the *Proceedings of the American Society of Civil Engineers* and *Living Light.*

Joseph A. Galante is bishop of Camden. He was auxiliary bishop of San Antonio, bishop of Beaumont, and coadjutor bishop of Dallas. He also served in Rome as undersecretary of the Congregation for Religious. In 2004, he was named bishop of Camden.

Daniel G. Groody, CSC, is assistant professor of theology and director of the Center for Latino Spirituality at Notre Dame. He is the author of *Border of Death, Valley of Life: An Immigrant Journey of Heart and Spirit* and *Globalization, Spirituality, and Justice: Navigating the Path to Peace* and is executive producer of the award-winning documentary film *Dying to Live: A Migrant's Journey.*

Thomas J. Gumbleton is auxiliary bishop of Detroit and former pastor of St. Leo's Parish. He is founding bishop-president of Pax Christi USA. As a leading voice for peace and justice, he has traveled around the world, including Afghanistan, Colombia, El Salvador, Guatemala, Haiti, Iraq, Iran, Nicaragua, and Peru.

Gustavo Gutiérrez, OP, pastor and theologian, is a native of Peru and the John Cardinal O'Hara Professor of Theology at the University of Notre

Dame. He is the author of numerous works, including the classic *A Theology of Liberation: History, Politics, and Salvation,* and is acknowledged as the "father of liberation theology."

Diana L. Hayes is a professor of theology at Georgetown University. She is the author of several books, including *Hagar's Daughters: Womanist Ways of Being in the World, And Still We Rise: An Introduction to Black Liberation Theology,* and *Were You There? Stations of the Cross* (with Charles S. Ndege).

John P. Hogan was associate director of the Peace Corps. He has lived and worked in Africa, South America, Haiti, and China. He has written on religion and social change and Catholic social teaching, including *Credible Signs of Christ Alive: Case Studies from the Catholic Campaign for Human Development.*

Robert T. McDermott, a Camden native, is pastor of Saint Joseph's Pro-Cathedral and vicar-general of the diocese of Camden. He is a founding organizer of the Romero Center, Saint Joseph's Carpenter Society, and Camden Churches Organized for People.

Helen Prejean, CSJ, is a noted speaker and writer. Her book *Dead Man Walking* was a best-seller and became an Oscar-winning film. She was nominated for a Pulitzer Prize and is the leading voice in the United States for abolition of the death penalty. In 2005, she authored *The Death of Innocents.*